Mathematics for Christian Living Series

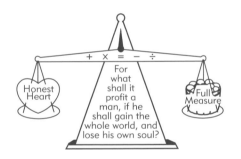

For what shall it profit a man, if he shall gain the whole world, and lose his own soul?

Honest Heart

Full Measure

Mathematics for Christian Living Series

Working Arithmetic

Grade 2

Unit 4, Lessons 103–137

Rod and Staff Publishers, Inc.

P.O. Box 3, Hwy. 172

Crockett, Kentucky 41413

Telephone: (606) 522-4348

Acknowledgments

We are indebted to God for the vision of the need for a *Mathematics for Christian Living Series* and for His enabling grace. Charitable contributions from many churches have helped to cover the expenses for research and development.

This revision was written by Sisters Miriam Rudolph and Marla Martin. The brethren Marvin Eicher, Jerry Kreider, and Luke Sensenig served as editors. Most of the illustrations were drawn by Lois Myer. The work was evaluated by a panel of reviewers and tested by teachers in the classroom. Much effort was devoted to the production of the book. We are grateful for all who helped to make this book possible.

—The Publishers

This book is part of a course for grade 2 arithmetic and will be most effective if used with the other parts of the course. *Working Arithmetic* includes the following items:

Teacher's Manual, part 1 (Units 1, 2)
Teacher's Manual, part 2 (Units 3–5)
Pupil's Workbook, Unit 1
Pupil's Workbook, Unit 2
Pupil's Workbook, Unit 3
Pupil's Workbook, Unit 4
Pupil's Workbook, Unit 5
Blacklines

Copyright 1992

by

Rod and Staff Publishers, Inc.
Crockett, Kentucky 41413

Printed in U.S.A.

ISBN 978-07399-0457-2

Catalog no. 13224.3

16   17   —   22   21   20   19

Unit 4 Contents

This list shows what concepts are introduced in these lessons. Each concept is also reviewed in following lessons.

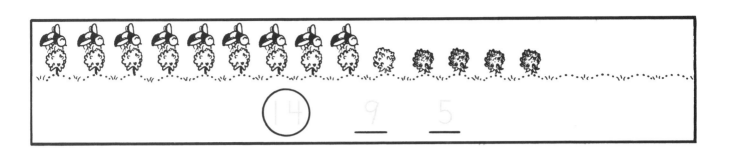

14 9 5

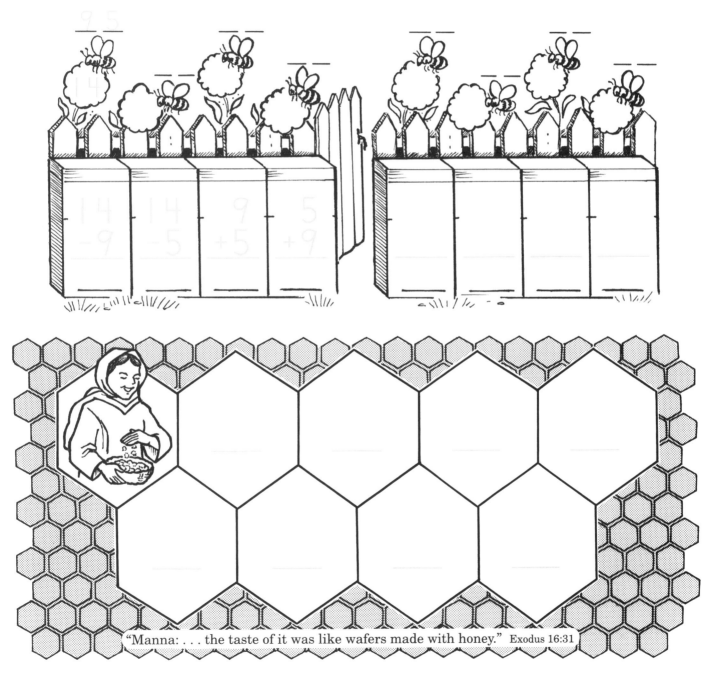

14   14   9   5
-9   -5   +5   +9
___ ___ ___ ___

"Manna: . . . the taste of it was like wafers made with honey." Exodus 16:31

7

14	14	14	14	9	14	14	9
−9	−5	−9	−5	+5	−9	−5	+5

5	14	9	5	14	5	14	14
+9	−9	+5	+9	−5	+9	−9	−9

14	14	5	14	5	9	14	9
−5	−9	+9	−9	+9	+5	−9	+5

5	9	14	5	14	14	9	14
+9	+5	−5	+9	−9	−5	+5	−5

14	14	14	14	14	14	14	5
−9	−5	−9	−5	−9	−9	−5	+9

9	14	14	14	5	14
+5	−9	−5	−5	+9	−9

93 -77	99 -76	93 -36	92 -65	77 -47	93 -55
98 -20	89 -37	73 -34	99 -78	72 -46	63 -39
62 -24	83 -26	57 -34	95 -65	62 -35	53 -37

Write $\frac{1}{2}$ on each **half**.

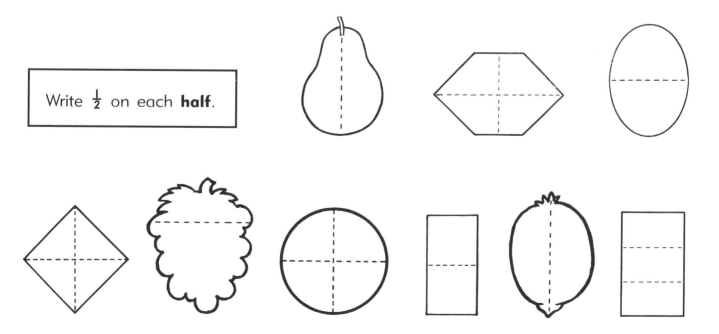

If it's **1** child on a swing
Or **14** bees on wing,
*"his eye
seeth
every
precious
thing."*

*Job
28:10*

If it's **100** cubs born new
Or **200** drops of dew,
*"his eye
seeth
every
precious
thing."*

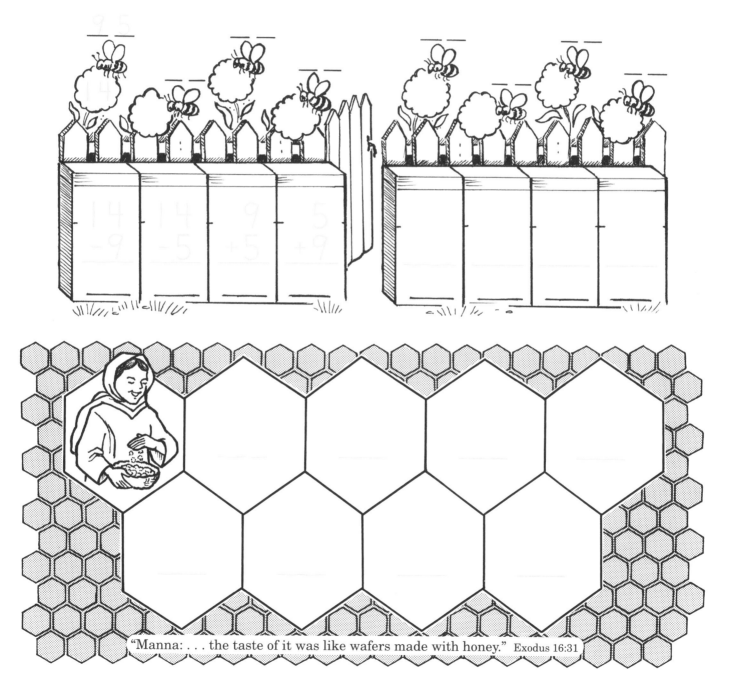

"Manna: . . . the taste of it was like wafers made with honey."   Exodus 16:31

14 −5	14 −9	14 −5	14 −5	9 +5	14 −5	14 −9	5 +9

9 +5	14 −9	5 +9	5 +9	14 −5	9 +5	14 −9	14 −5

14 −9	14 −5	5 +9	14 −9	5 +9	9 +5	14 −5	9 +5

9 +5	5 +9	14 −5	5 +9	14 −9	14 −5	9 +5	14 −9

14 −5	14 −5	14 −9	14 −5	9 +5	14 −9	14 −5	5 +9

9 +5	5 +9	14 −5	14 −5	5 +9	14 −5

43	14	56	24	74	35
34	23	12	14	15	43
+62	+94	+61	+95	+42	+34

55	34	61	35	52	44
32	42	25	43	37	23
+25	+55	+47	+51	+42	+72

14	9	14	5	5	14
-5	+5	-9	+9	+9	-5

14	14	9	5	14	14
-9	-5	+5	+9	-9	-5

14	5	14	9	5	14	9	14
-9	+9	-5	+5	+9	-9	+5	-5

9	14	14	14	9	5	14	14
+5	-9	-5	-9	+5	+9	-5	-9

"Whatsoever thy hand findeth to do, do it with thy might." Ecclesiastes 9:10

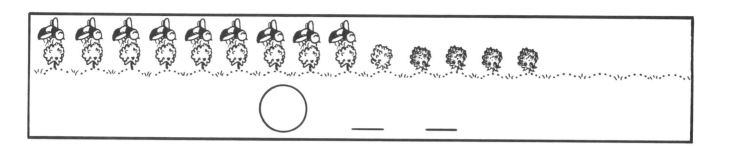

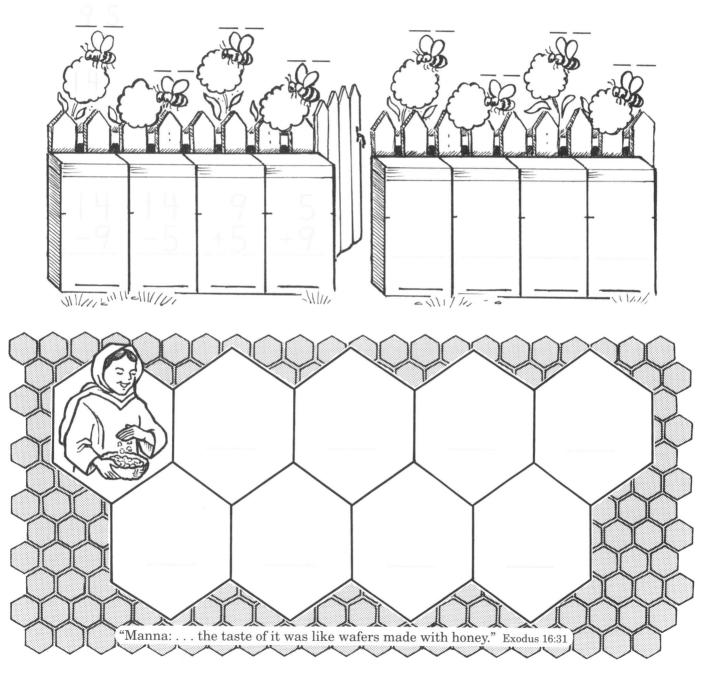

"Manna: . . . the taste of it was like wafers made with honey." Exodus 16:31

144 −93	35 +49	147 −55	146 −94	96 +53	148 −56
35 +69	149 −56	85 +55	149 −94	35 +29	147 −54
59 +25	149 −98	144 −92	145 −53	149 −57	94 +55
148 −55	59 +45	147 −92	90 +50	146 −53	39 +25
145 −95	52 +92	148 −54	75 +29	84 +56	149 −58
		89 +15	147 −53	91 +53	147 −97

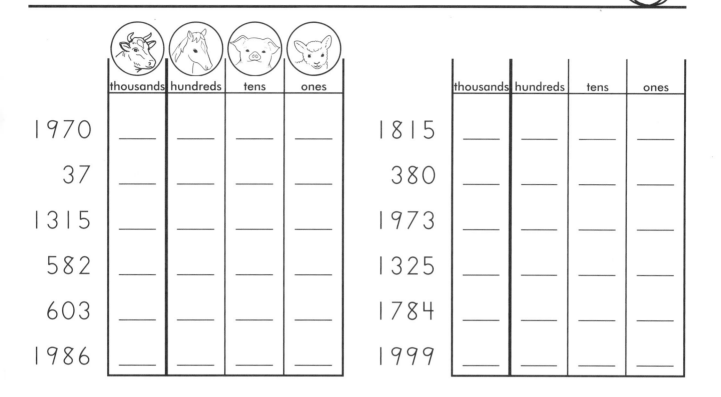

	thousands	hundreds	tens	ones
1970	___	___	___	___
37	___	___	___	___
1315	___	___	___	___
582	___	___	___	___
603	___	___	___	___
1986	___	___	___	___

	thousands	hundreds	tens	ones
1815	___	___	___	___
380	___	___	___	___
1973	___	___	___	___
1325	___	___	___	___
1784	___	___	___	___
1999	___	___	___	___

14 deer made tracks in the snow. Five deer were big, but the rest were small. How many deer were small?

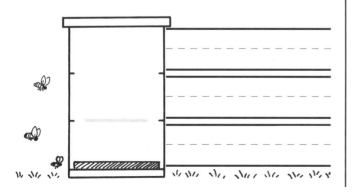

13 birds eat at a bird feeder. Six birds are red, and the rest are brown. How many birds are brown?

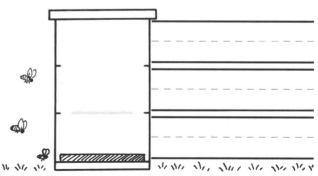

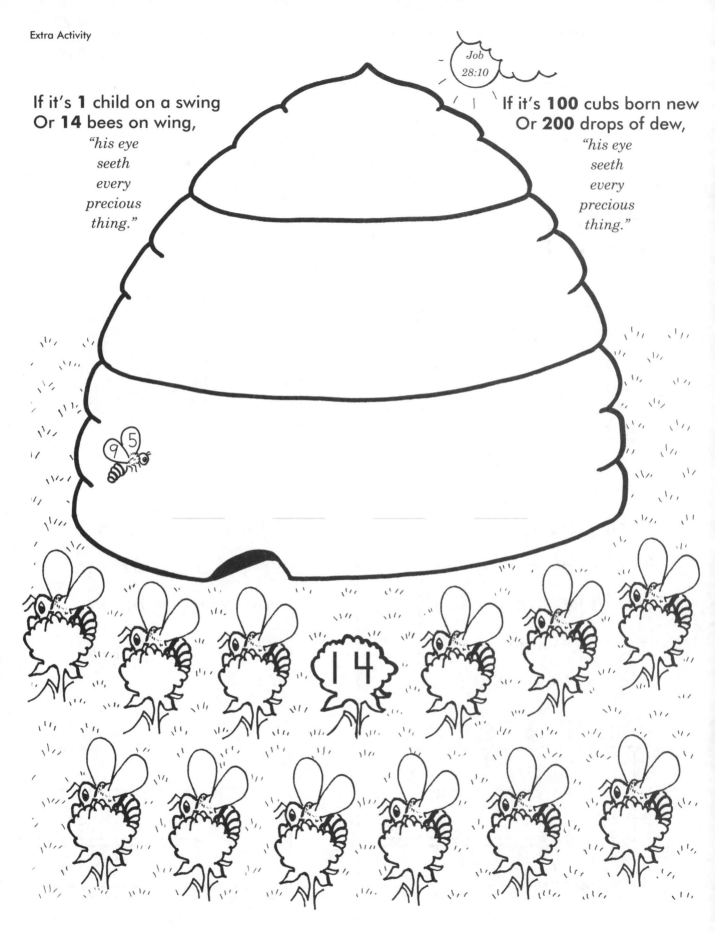

If it's **1** child on a swing
Or **14** bees on wing,

"his eye seeth every precious thing."

Job 28:10

If it's **100** cubs born new
Or **200** drops of dew,

"his eye seeth every precious thing."

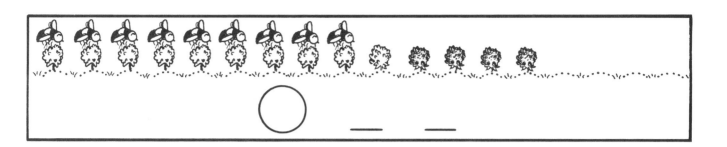

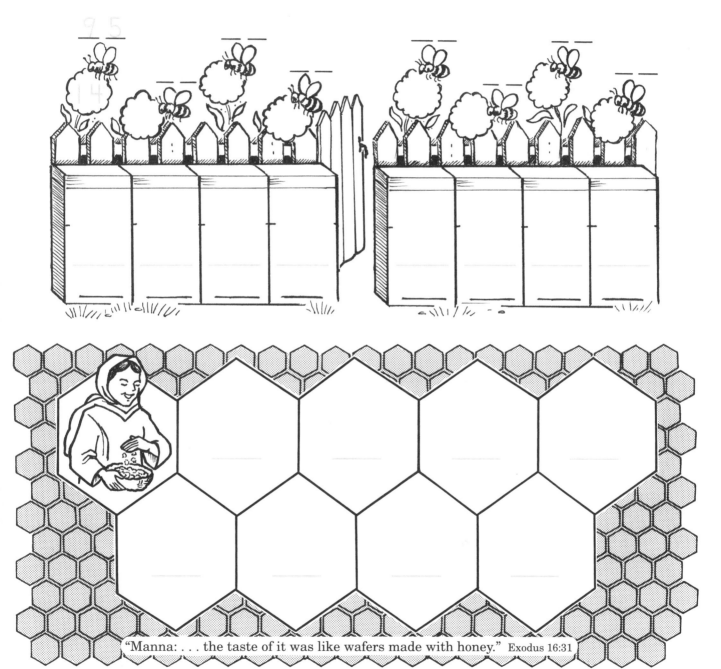

"Manna: . . . the taste of it was like wafers made with honey." Exodus 16:31

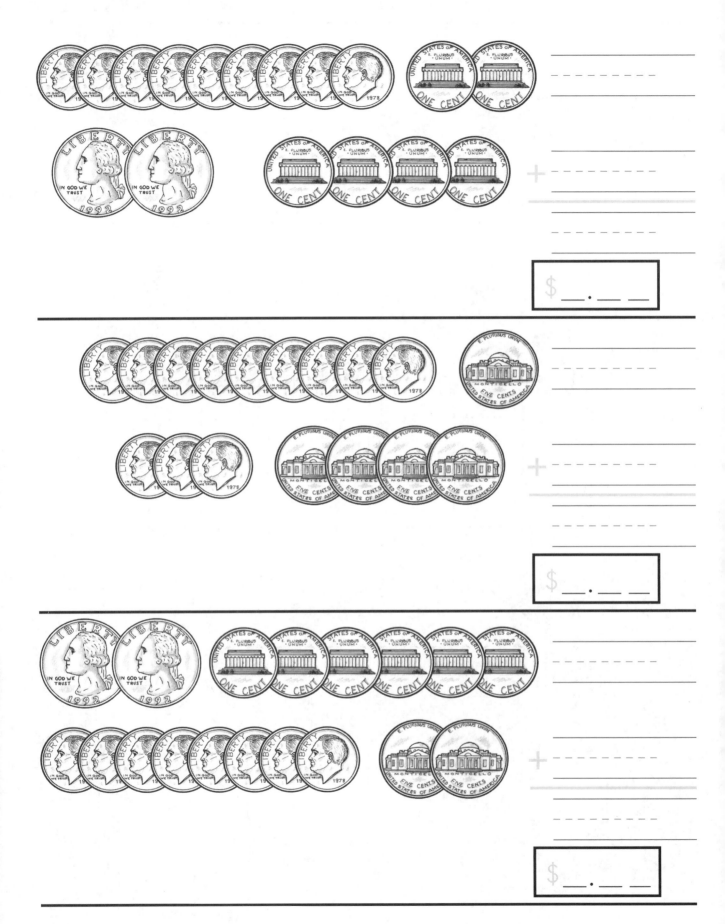

$ __ . __ __

$ __ . __ __

$ __ . __ __

94	55	83	53	83	94
-55	+94	-47	-29	+55	-29

53	96	73	93	76	83
-18	+52	-39	-67	+63	-14

94	83	93	94	74	67
+44	-35	-36	-19	-25	+72

14	13	14	13	9	13	13	5
-9	-9	-5	-8	+5	-4	-9	+9

7	13	8	9	14	6	13	14
+6	-7	+5	+4	-5	+7	-7	-5

14	13	4	13	5	14
-5	-4	+9	-9	+9	-9

13	13	14	14	9	9
-9	-4	-5	-9	+5	+4

9	13	14	5	13	9	13	14
+5	-4	-9	+9	-9	+4	-4	-5

14	5	4	9	14	13	14	13
-5	+9	+9	+5	-9	-4	-5	-9

"Whatsoever thy hand findeth to do, do it with thy might." Ecclesiastes 9:10

"Manna: . . . the taste of it was like wafers made with honey." Exodus 16:31

$9 + \underline{} = 14$	$14 - \underline{} = 5$	$\underline{} - 5 = 9$
$5 + \underline{} = 14$	$\underline{} + 9 = 14$	$5 + \underline{} = 14$
$14 - \underline{} = 5$	$\underline{} - 9 = 5$	$14 - 9 = \underline{}$
$14 - \underline{} = 9$	$14 - 5 = \underline{}$	$\underline{} - 5 = 9$
$\underline{} + 9 = 14$	$5 + \underline{} = 14$	$5 + \underline{} = 14$
$\underline{} - 9 = 5$	$9 + 5 = \underline{}$	$\underline{} - 9 = 5$

$$
\begin{array}{cccccccc}
6 & 3 & 6 & 4 & 8 & 5 & 7 & 3 \\
3 & 2 & 2 & 5 & 1 & 2 & 2 & 2 \\
+5 & +9 & +4 & +2 & +5 & +6 & +5 & +9 \\
\hline
\end{array}
$$

$$
\begin{array}{cccccccc}
5 & 2 & 2 & 4 & 6 & 1 & 1 & 5 \\
4 & 3 & 7 & 1 & 3 & 8 & 4 & 0 \\
+5 & +9 & +4 & +9 & +2 & +3 & +9 & +9 \\
\hline
\end{array}
$$

	thousands	hundreds	tens	ones
1893	___	___	___	___
306	___	___	___	___
1929	___	___	___	___
93	___	___	___	___
1945	___	___	___	___
1784	___	___	___	___
623	___	___	___	___

	thousands	hundreds	tens	ones
897	___	___	___	___
1582	___	___	___	___
607	___	___	___	___
1315	___	___	___	___
1290	___	___	___	___
324	___	___	___	___
1918	___	___	___	___

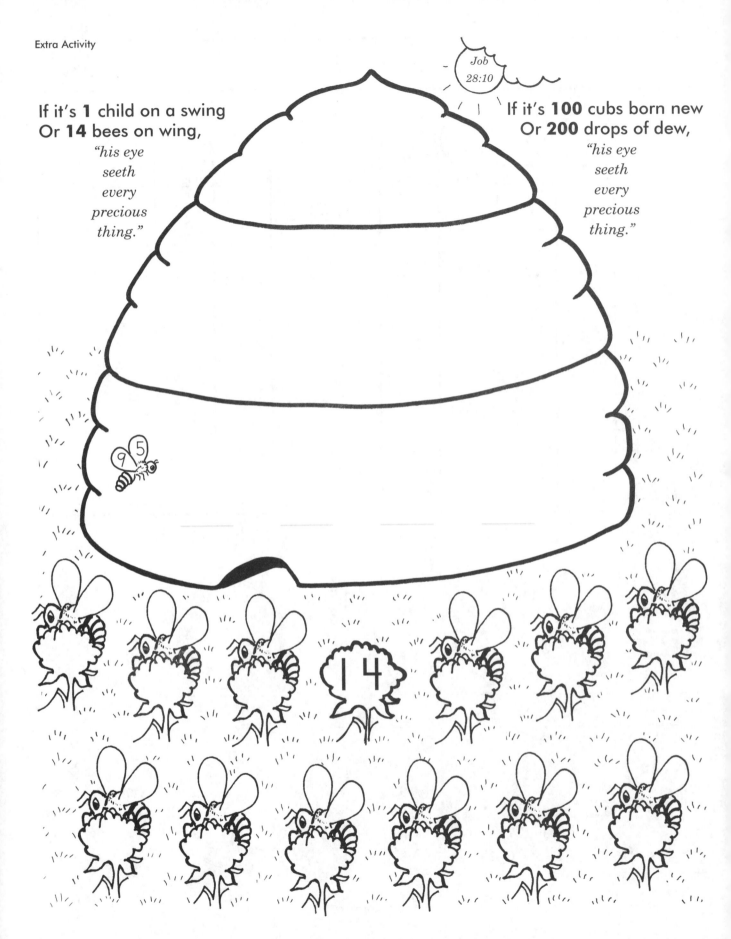

If it's **1** child on a swing
Or **14** bees on wing,

"his eye
seeth
every
precious
thing."

Job 28:10

If it's **100** cubs born new
Or **200** drops of dew,

"his eye
seeth
every
precious
thing."

"Manna: . . . the taste of it was like wafers made with honey." Exodus 16:31

Mark fed fourteen cows for Father. Nine cows were brown. The rest were black. How many cows were black?

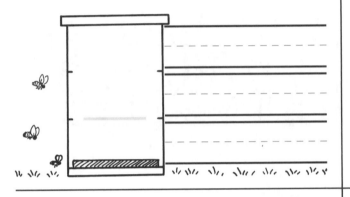

Father went to visit a new church. He drove five days to get to the church. He stayed 9 days to preach. How many days was that altogether?

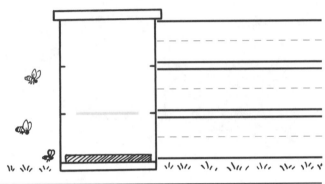

Lois peels thirteen apples for Mother. 7 apples are red, and the rest are yellow. How many apples are yellow?

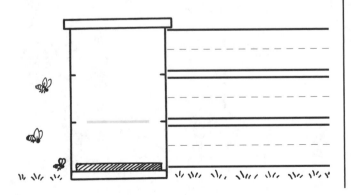

Father has fourteen hives for bees. A bear opens 5 hives. How many hives does the bear not open?

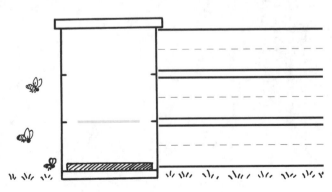

94	73	99	74	94	93
-59	-57	+50	+63	-45	-69

53	94	92	83	53	73
+90	-69	+52	-57	+92	-46

82	93	53	55	82	83
-46	-78	+94	+84	-38	-54

Write ¼ on each **fourth**.

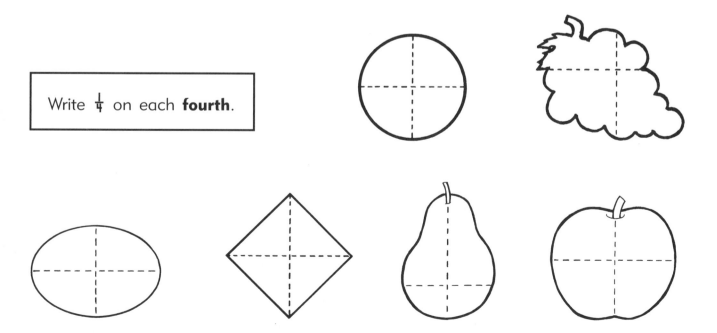

13	14	13	11	13	13
-8	-5	-5	-7	-6	-7

12	12	12	14	11	14
-8	-4	-5	-5	-5	-9

12	14	13	13	13	11	12	13
-5	-5	-7	-6	-9	-3	-3	-8

14	13	14	12	13	11	13	13
-5	-6	-9	-6	-4	-4	-5	-9

"Whatsoever thy hand findeth to do, do it with thy might." Ecclesiastes 9:10

$$9 \quad 5$$
$$14$$

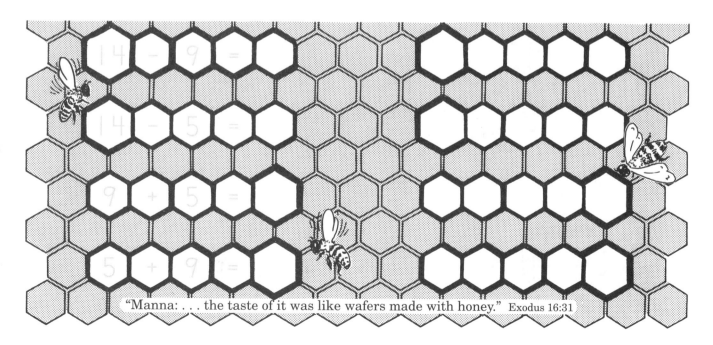

$$14 - 9 =$$

$$14 - 5 =$$

$$9 + 5 =$$

$$5 + 9 =$$

"Manna: . . . the taste of it was like wafers made with honey." Exodus 16:31

14	13	14	14	9	14	13	4
-5	-4	-9	-5	+4	-9	-4	+9

9	13	9	4	14	5	13	14
+4	-9	+5	+9	-5	+9	-9	-5

13	14	4	13	5	9	14	9
-9	-9	+9	-9	+9	+4	-9	+4

4	9	13	5	13	13	9	13
+9	+5	-4	+9	-9	-4	+5	-9

13	14	14	14	14	14	14	5
-4	-5	-9	-5	-9	-9	-5	+9

9	14	14	14	5	13
+5	-9	-5	-5	+9	-4

$$\begin{array}{r} 94 \\ -79 \\ \hline \end{array}$$
$$\begin{array}{r} 73 \\ -26 \\ \hline \end{array}$$
$$\begin{array}{r} 74 \\ +63 \\ \hline \end{array}$$
$$\begin{array}{r} 53 \\ +96 \\ \hline \end{array}$$
$$\begin{array}{r} 94 \\ -69 \\ \hline \end{array}$$
$$\begin{array}{r} 93 \\ -27 \\ \hline \end{array}$$

$$\begin{array}{r} 90 \\ +52 \\ \hline \end{array}$$
$$\begin{array}{r} 73 \\ -15 \\ \hline \end{array}$$
$$\begin{array}{r} 50 \\ +90 \\ \hline \end{array}$$
$$\begin{array}{r} 83 \\ -27 \\ \hline \end{array}$$
$$\begin{array}{r} 62 \\ +76 \\ \hline \end{array}$$
$$\begin{array}{r} 83 \\ -29 \\ \hline \end{array}$$

$$\begin{array}{r} 82 \\ -65 \\ \hline \end{array}$$
$$\begin{array}{r} 84 \\ -39 \\ \hline \end{array}$$
$$\begin{array}{r} 54 \\ +85 \\ \hline \end{array}$$
$$\begin{array}{r} 93 \\ +54 \\ \hline \end{array}$$
$$\begin{array}{r} 82 \\ -56 \\ \hline \end{array}$$
$$\begin{array}{r} 84 \\ -19 \\ \hline \end{array}$$

Write $\frac{1}{4}$ on each **fourth**.

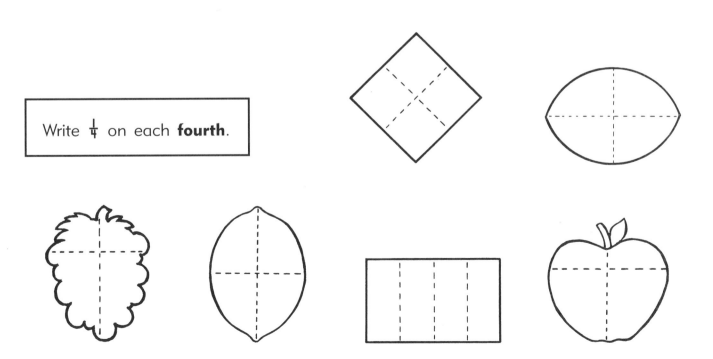

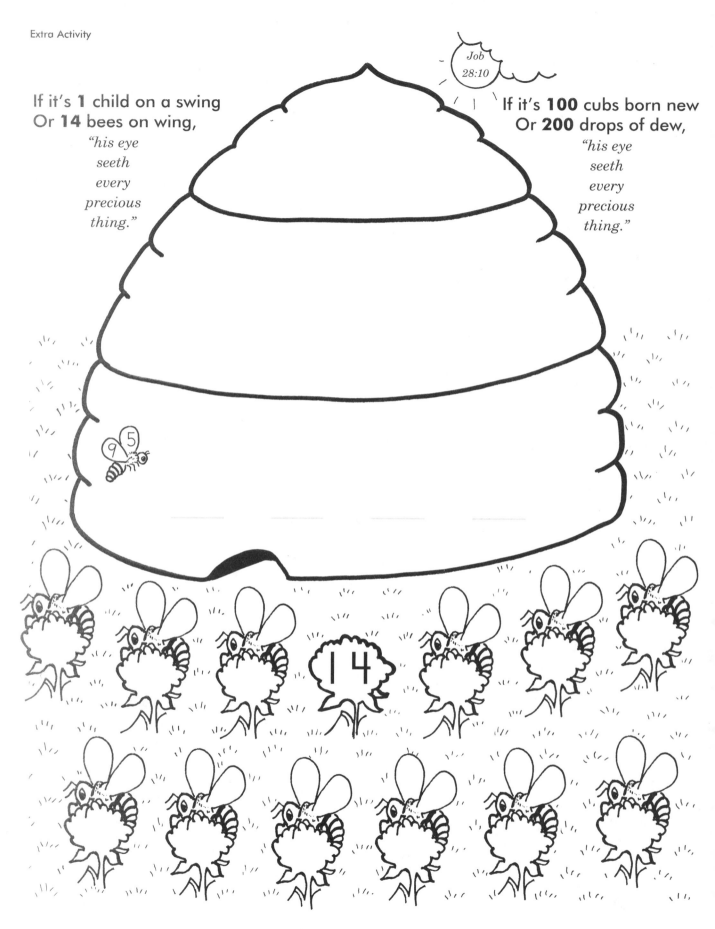

If it's **1** child on a swing
Or **14** bees on wing,

*"his eye
seeth
every
precious
thing."*

*Job
28:10*

If it's **100** cubs born new
Or **200** drops of dew,

*"his eye
seeth
every
precious
thing."*

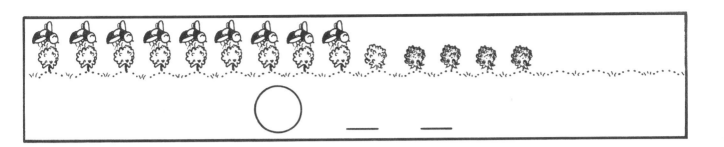

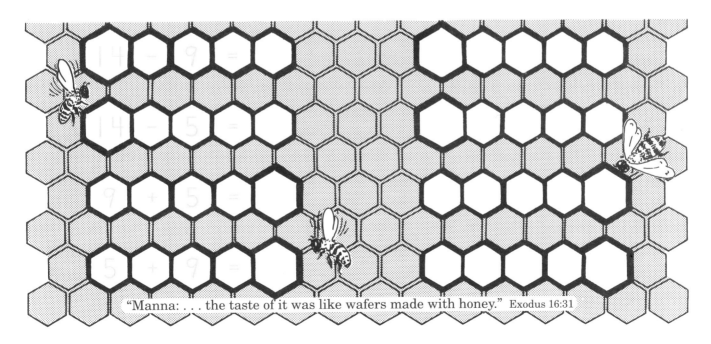

"Manna: . . . the taste of it was like wafers made with honey." Exodus 16:31

14	13	12	14	7	11	12	6
-9	-7	-8	-5	+6	-7	-6	+5

4	13	9	9	14	5	11	14
+7	-8	+5	+4	-5	+9	-6	-9

12	14	5	13	8	3	14	5
-9	-9	+6	-5	+4	+8	-9	+7

4	7	13	3	12	13	6	11
+8	+5	-9	+9	-4	-9	+6	-8

13	13	12	14	11	13	12	5
-6	-8	3	-5	-5	-4	-7	+8

4	13	14	12	6	11
+9	-7	-5	-5	+7	-4

89 +55	96 −73	47 +96	53 +76	96 −54	99 −38
53 +79	89 −21	69 +65	80 −10	62 +74	98 −26
46 +97	88 −64	94 +55	35 +88	78 −37	87 −25

Write ¼ on each **fourth**.

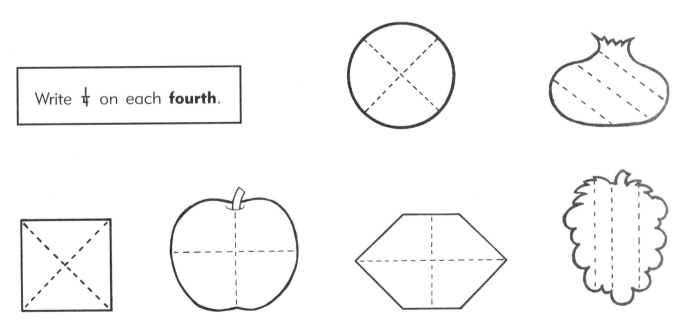

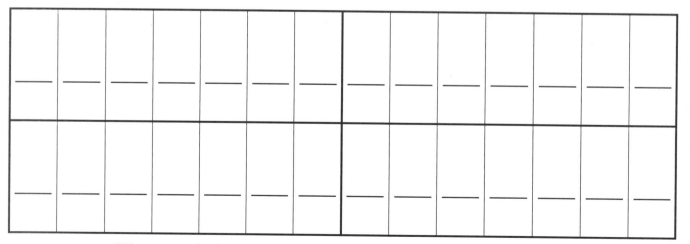

Speed Drill

5	8	8	9	5	8
+9	+5	+5	+5	+8	+5

9	9	5	8	9	5
+5	+5	+9	+5	+5	+9

5	5	5	8	9	5	8	5
+9	+8	+8	+5	+5	+8	+5	+9

5	2	3	4	2	3	2	7
4	7	2	5	6	6	3	2
+4	+5	+9	+5	+5	+5	+9	+5

"Whatsoever thy hand findeth to do, do it with thy might." Ecclesiastes 9:10

38

14   8   6

| 14 | 14 | 8 | 6 |
| -8 | -6 | +6 | +8 |

"Manna: . . . the taste of it was like wafers made with honey." Exodus 16:31

14	14	14	14	6	14	14	8
-8	-6	-8	-6	+8	-8	-6	+6

6	14	6	8	14	8	14	14
+8	-6	+8	+6	-6	+6	-6	-8

14	14	8	14	8	6	14	6
-6	-8	+6	-8	+6	+8	-8	+8

6	8	14	6	14	14	6	14
+8	+6	-6	+8	-8	-6	+8	-6

14	14	14	14	8	14	14	8
-8	-6	-8	-6	+6	-8	-6	+6

8	6	14	14	6	14
+6	+8	-6	-6	+8	-8

94 -79	73 -26	49 +35	44 +29	93 -67	93 -28
29 +54	73 -15	59 +34	83 -27	36 +67	83 -29
82 -35	84 -69	25 +48	45 +39	82 -56	84 -19

Write $\frac{1}{4}$ on each **fourth**.

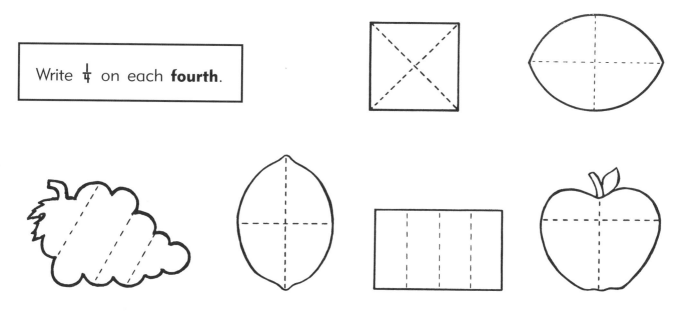

41

If it's **1** child on a swing
Or **14** bees on wing,

"his eye
seeth
every
precious
thing."

Job 28:10

If it's **100** cubs born new
Or **200** drops of dew,

"his eye
seeth
every
precious
thing."

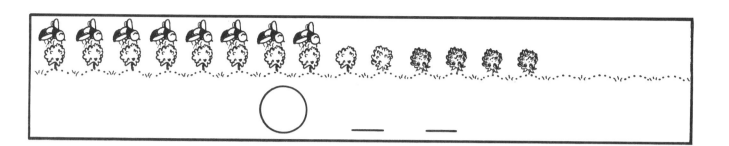

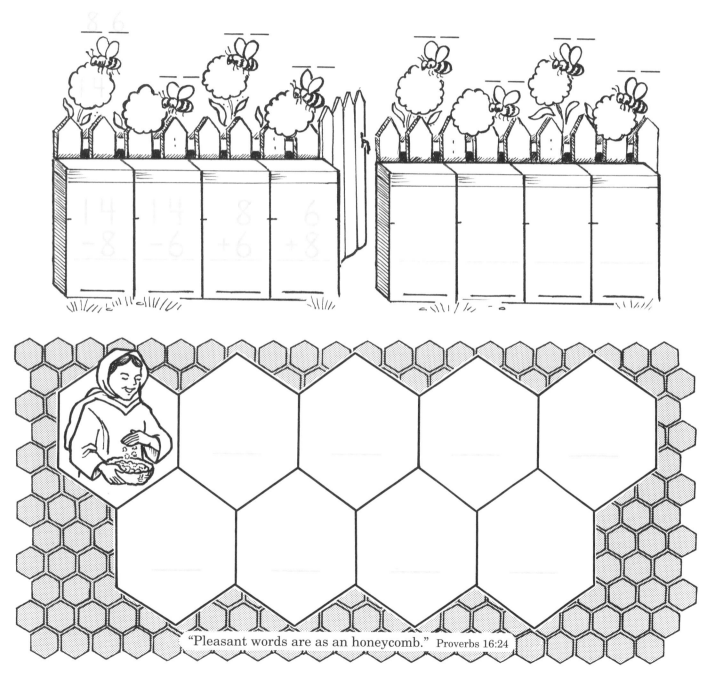

"Pleasant words are as an honeycomb." Proverbs 16:24

14 −6	14 −8	14 −6	14 −6	6 +8	14 −6	14 −8	6 +8
8 +6	14 −8	6 +8	8 +6	14 −6	8 +6	14 −8	14 −6
14 −6	14 −8	8 +6	14 −8	8 +6	6 +8	14 −8	6 +8
6 +8	8 +6	14 −6	6 +8	14 −8	14 −6	6 +8	14 −6
14 −8	14 −6	14 −8	14 −6	8 +6	14 −8	14 −6	8 +6
			8 +6	6 +8	14 −6	14 −6	6 +8	14 −8

```
  74        52        56        24        43        55
  15        37        12        14        34        32
 +42       +42       +61       +95       +62       +25
_____     _____     _____     _____     _____     _____


  35        44        61        35        14        34
  43        23        25        43        23        42
 + 4       + 2       + 7       + 1       + 4       + 5
_____     _____     _____     _____     _____     _____
```

Fay was sick in bed. On Friday 17 cards came for her in the mail. On Saturday 16 cards came. How many cards was that in all?

Fred found fourteen shells by the sea. Nine shells were brown. The rest were white. How many shells were white?

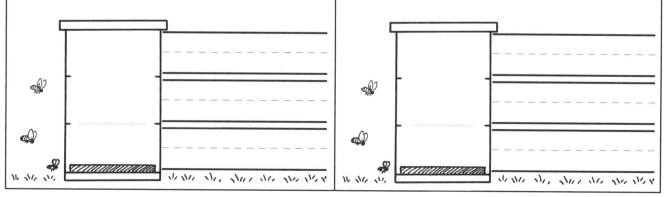

45

14	6	8	14	14	14
-8	+8	+6	-6	-8	-6

8	14	6	14	14	8
+6	-6	+8	-8	-6	+6

14	6	14	14	14	8	6	14
-6	+8	-6	-8	-6	+6	+8	-8

6	14	8	14	14	6	14	8
+8	-6	+6	-6	-8	+8	-6	+6

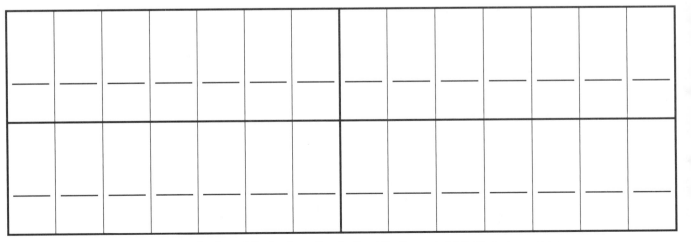

"Whatsoever thy hand findeth to do, do it with thy might." Ecclesiastes 9:10

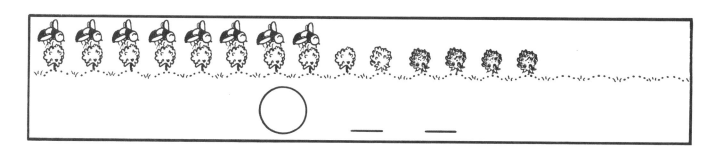

"Pleasant words are as an honeycomb." Proverbs 16:24

148	58	147	146	66	148
-84	+26	-64	-84	+82	-66

76	149	75	149	28	147
+18	-86	+65	-64	+76	-84

36	146	144	148	149	83
+48	-82	-82	-65	-67	+65

148	58	147	60	146	56
-85	+36	-62	+80	-83	+48

149	83	148	78	74	148
-82	+66	-64	+26	+66	-65

46	147	64	148
+58	-63	+85	-81

	thousands	hundreds	tens	ones
1984	___	___	___	___
815	___	___	___	___
1945	___	___	___	___
16	___	___	___	___
1625	___	___	___	___
1784	___	___	___	___
1315	___	___	___	___

	thousands	hundreds	tens	ones
584	___	___	___	___
1623	___	___	___	___
80	___	___	___	___
1415	___	___	___	___
293	___	___	___	___
1324	___	___	___	___
1583	___	___	___	___

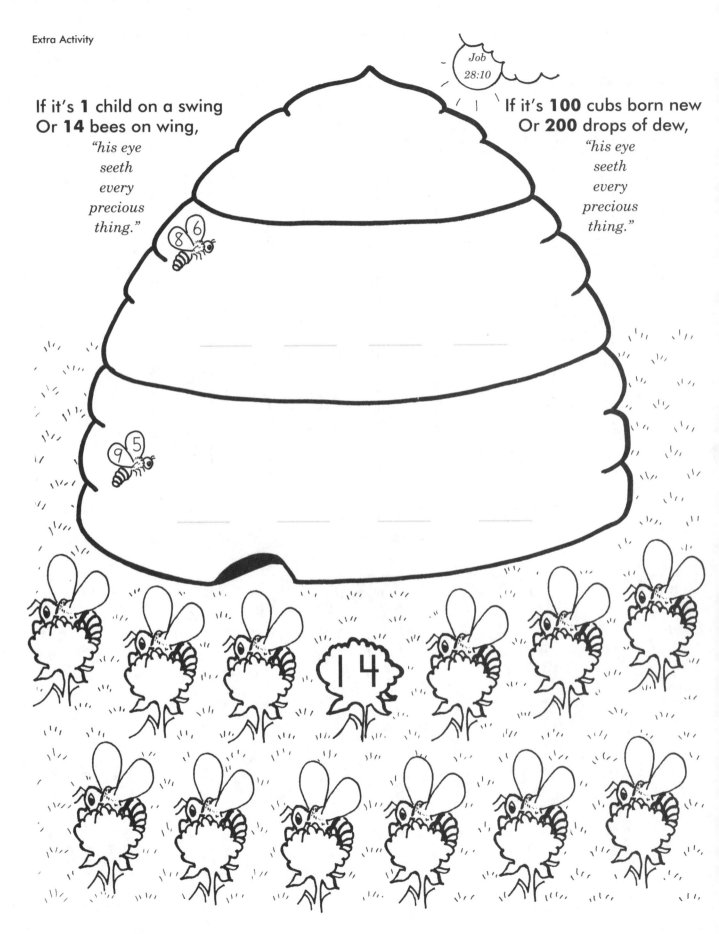

If it's **1** child on a swing
Or **14** bees on wing,

*"his eye
seeth
every
precious
thing."*

Job 28:10

If it's **100** cubs born new
Or **200** drops of dew,

*"his eye
seeth
every
precious
thing."*

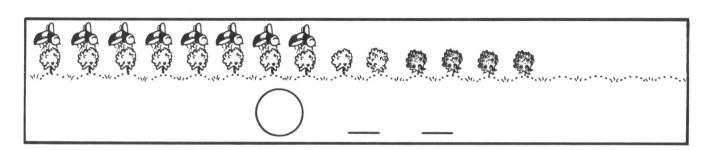

"Pleasant words are as an honeycomb." Proverbs 16:24

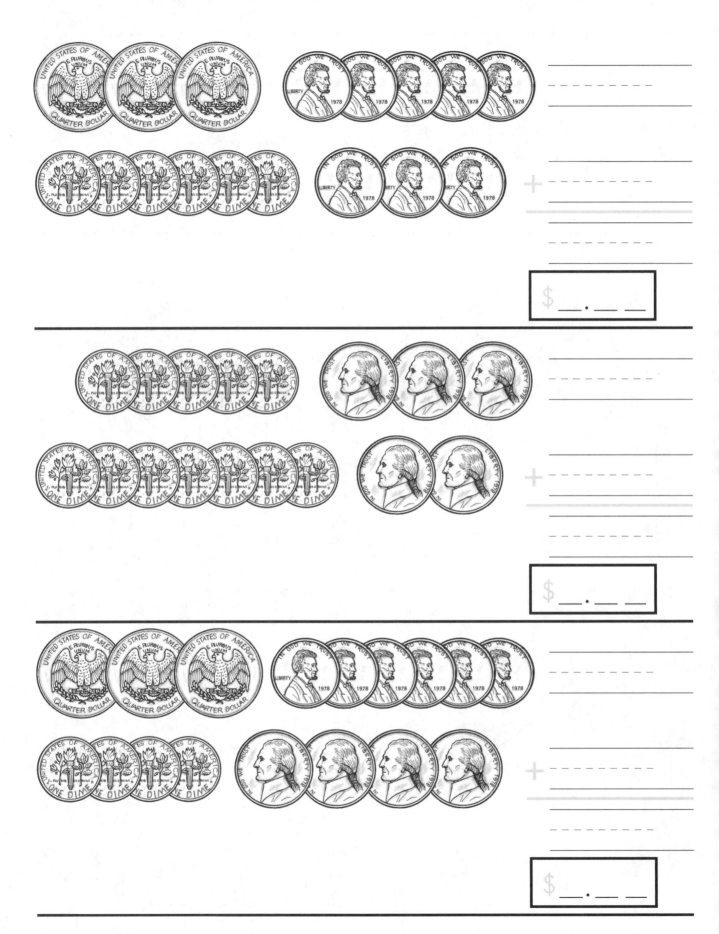

```
  89       94       47       56       94       84
 +55      -78      +96      +78      -56      -26
```

```
  53       35       69       93       84       94
 +79      +88      +55      +36      -16      -29
```

```
  46       84       46       68       74       82
 +97      -65      +87      +66      -36      -24
```

On Friday 16 men helped to paint the min-is-ter's house. On Saturday 18 men helped. How many men was that in all?

Father has 89 nails in a bag. He hammers 57 of the nails into a roof he is mending. How many nails are left in his bag?

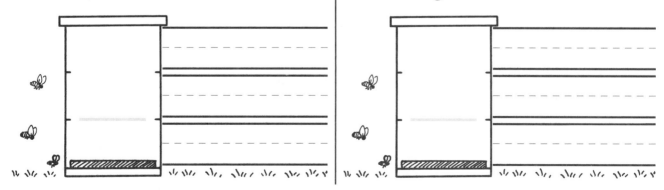

14 −6	14 −5	9 +5	14 −8	14 −9	6 +8

5 +9	8 +6	14 −8	14 −9	14 −6	9 +5

14 −8	5 +9	8 +6	14 −9	14 −8	6 +8	14 −5	14 −6

9 +5	14 −8	8 +6	14 −6	14 −9	14 −8	5 +9	6 +8

"Whatsoever thy hand findeth to do, do it with thy might." Ecclesiastes 9:10

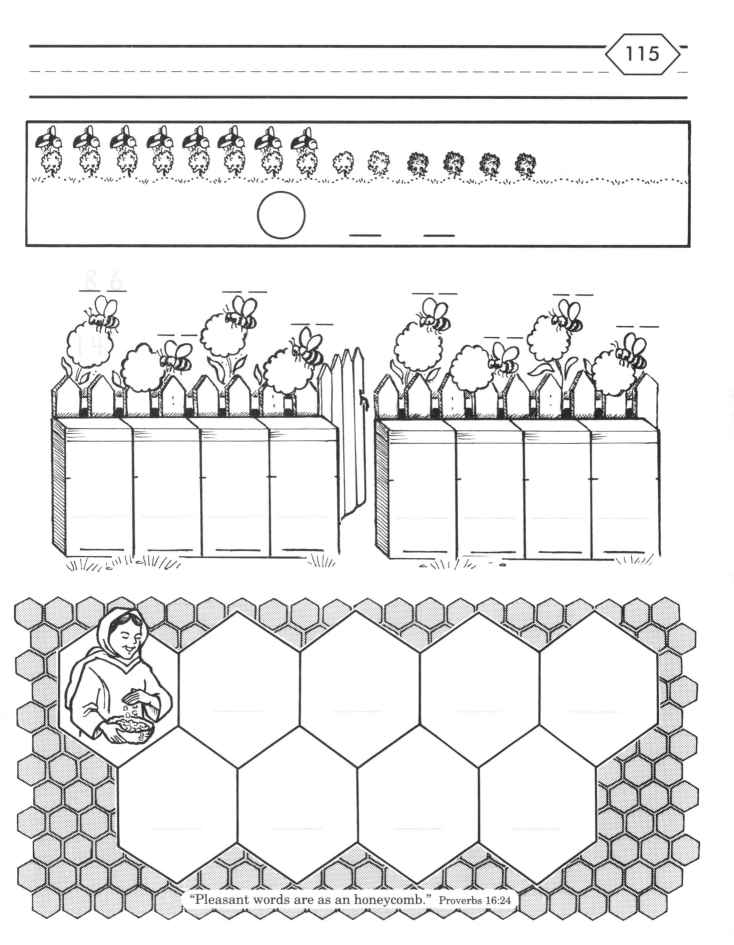

"Pleasant words are as an honeycomb." Proverbs 16:24

14 − 8 = ___	14 − ___ = 8	___ + 6 = 14
14 − 6 = ___	___ + 6 = 14	___ + 8 = 14
6 + ___ = 14	6 + 8 = ___	14 − ___ = 6
___ − 8 = 6	14 − ___ = 8	___ − 6 = 8
8 + ___ = 14	___ + 6 = 14	6 + 8 = ___
14 − ___ = 6	6 + 8 = ___	14 − ___ = 6

6	3	3	4	6	2	1	4
2	5	2	2	3	7	6	4
+6	+6	+8	+8	+4	+3	+3	+6
___	___	___	___	___	___	___	___

6	2	5	6	4	7	3	5
2	4	3	3	5	1	3	3
+5	+8	+6	+3	+4	+6	+8	+2
___	___	___	___	___	___	___	___

```
 583     328     256     489     168     458
+257    +596    +178    +354    +653    +184
-----   -----   -----   -----   -----   -----


 433     476     286     307     154     158
+268    +164    +248    +394    +486    +376
-----   -----   -----   -----   -----   -----


 259     223     578     145     266     456
+383    +598    +265    +289    +658    +384
-----   -----   -----   -----   -----   -----
```

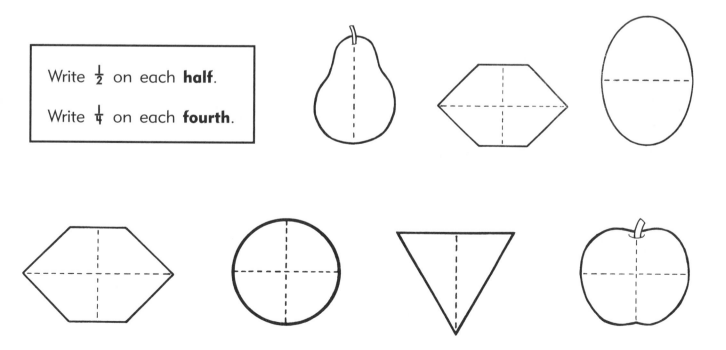

Write ½ on each **half**.

Write ¼ on each **fourth**.

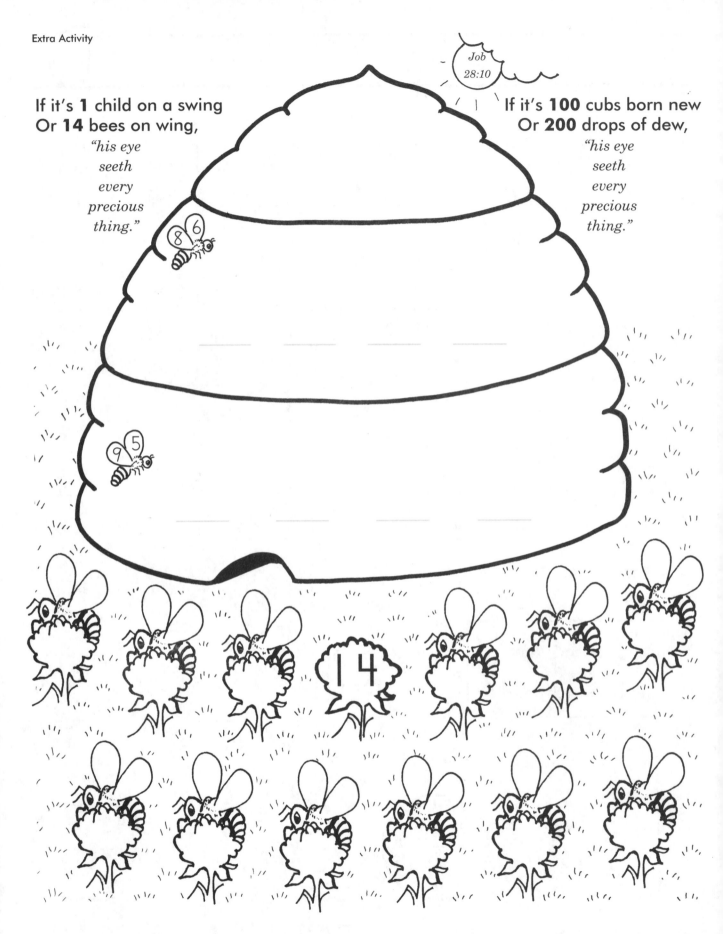

If it's **1** child on a swing
Or **14** bees on wing,

"his eye seeth every precious thing."

If it's **100** cubs born new
Or **200** drops of dew,

"his eye seeth every precious thing."

Job 28:10

8 6

14

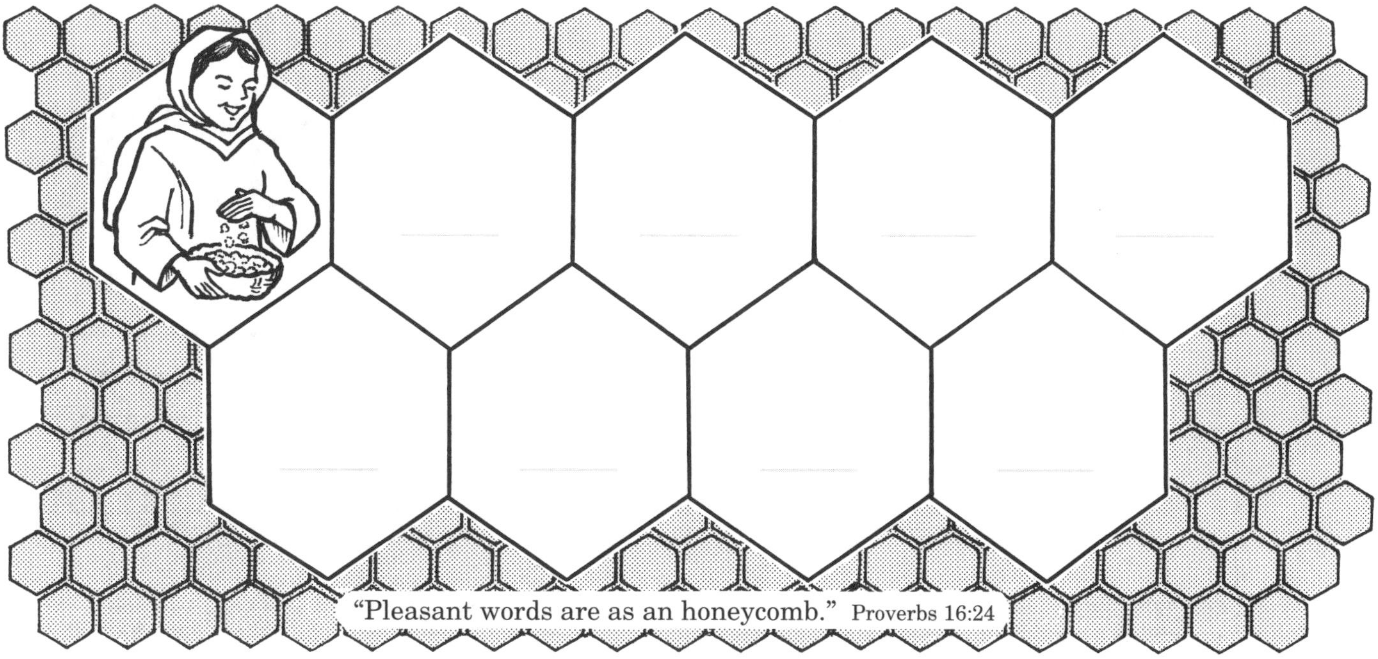

"Pleasant words are as an honeycomb." Proverbs 16:24

Father planted 14 trees. Six trees were pine. The rest were oak. How many trees were oak?

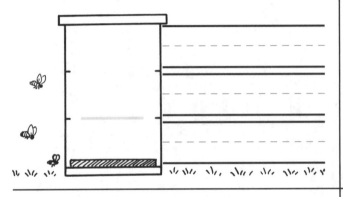

Fred gave 83¢ to the Lord's work. Lois gave 64¢. How many cents did both children give?

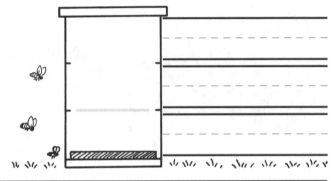

A flock of 89 geese swim on the lake. 57 geese fly up and away. How many geese are on the lake now?

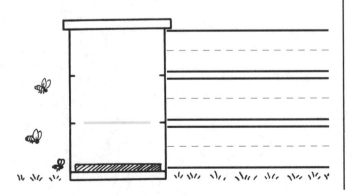

Fourteen goats eat grass. Eight goats have bells around their necks. How many goats do not have bells?

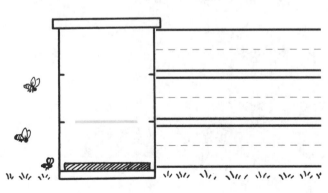

```
  287      528      256      489      168      658
 +654     +296     +578     +354     +553     +284
_____   _____   _____   _____   _____   _____


  483      376      286      357      554      158
 +258     +564     +248     +384     +586     +376
_____   _____   _____   _____   _____   _____


  456      523      558      345      366      755
 +486     +198     +285     +489     +458     +186
_____   _____   _____   _____   _____   _____
```

Write ½ on each **half**.

Write ¼ on each **fourth**.

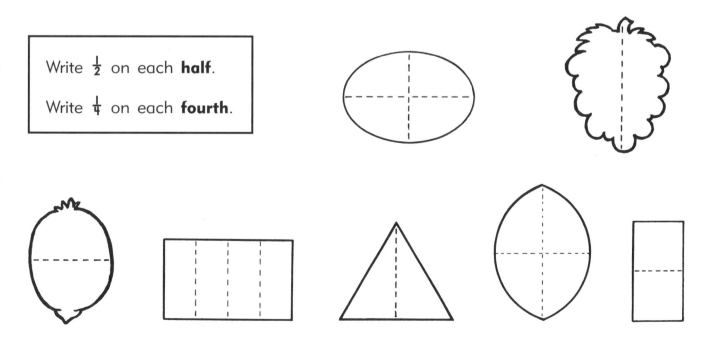

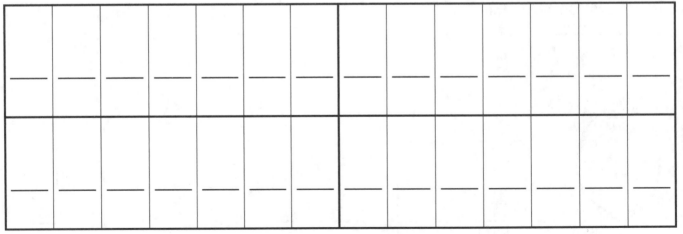

Speed Drill

8 +6	8 +5	14 -6	13 -5	6 +8	13 -8

13 -8	14 -6	8 +6	13 -5	8 +5	14 -8

14 -6	8 +5	13 -8	6 +8	14 -6	13 -5	8 +5	8 +6

8 +5	13 -5	14 -8	5 +8	13 -5	8 +6	14 -6	13 -8

"Whatsoever thy hand findeth to do, do it with thy might." Ecclesiastes 9:10

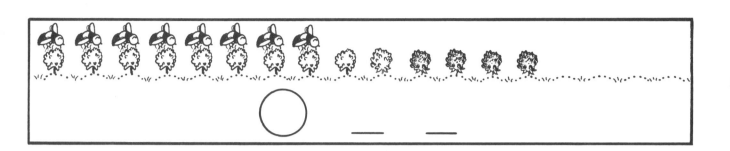

○   ___ ___

"Pleasant words are as an honeycomb." Proverbs 16:24

14 −8	14 −6	13 −5	13 −8	8 +6	13 −5	14 −6	8 +5
5 +8	14 −6	6 +8	8 +6	13 −8	8 +6	14 −6	14 −8
14 −8	13 −8	8 +5	14 −6	6 +8	8 +5	13 −8	5 +8
8 +5	6 +8	13 −5	8 +6	14 −6	13 −5	8 +6	14 −8
14 −8	13 −5	14 −8	14 −6	13 −8	14 −8	13 −5	8 +5
		5 +8	13 −8	14 −6	13 −5	8 +5	14 −8

```
  573      328      356      488      165      458
 +267     +596     +378     +356     +658     +184
 ─────    ─────    ─────    ─────    ─────    ─────


  433      276      286      307      354      158
 +268     +564     +248     +394     +486     +376
 ─────    ─────    ─────    ─────    ─────    ─────


  259      228      576      445      266      486
 +383     +595     +268     +289     +658     +354
 ─────    ─────    ─────    ─────    ─────    ─────
```

12 things = 1 dozen

6 things = ½ dozen

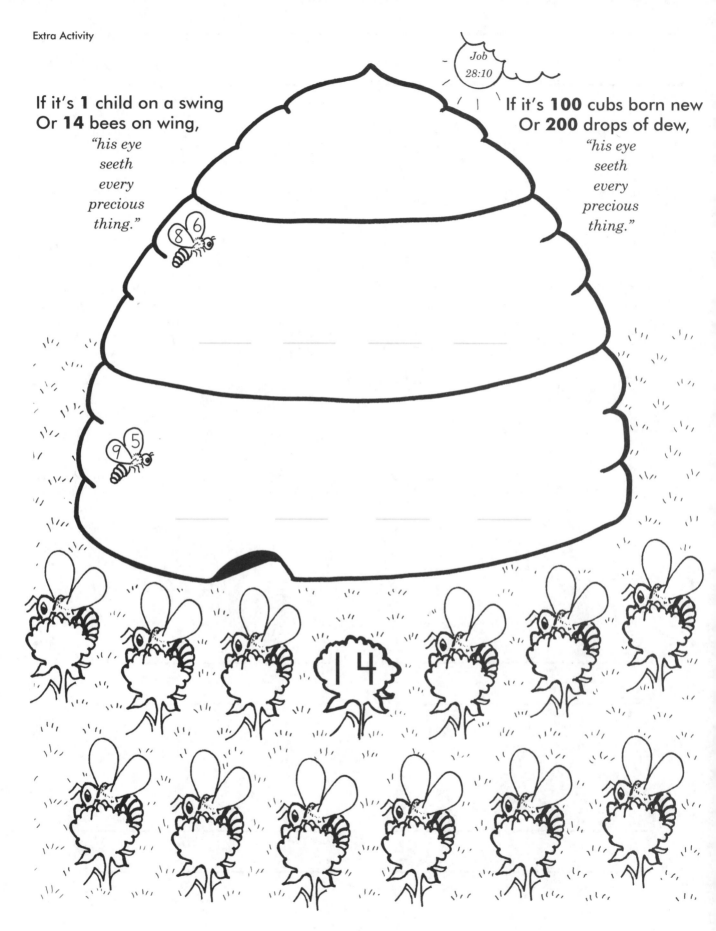

If it's **1** child on a swing
Or **14** bees on wing,

*"his eye
seeth
every
precious
thing."*

*Job
28:10*

If it's **100** cubs born new
Or **200** drops of dew,

*"his eye
seeth
every
precious
thing."*

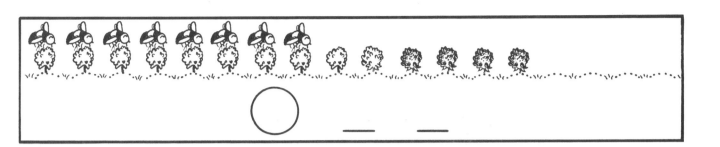

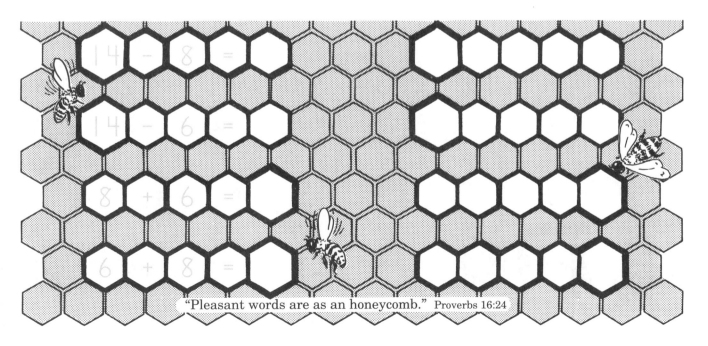

"Pleasant words are as an honeycomb." Proverbs 16:24

14 −8	14 −5	13 −5	12 −8	8 +6	14 −6	13 −4	9 +3

8 +4	14 −9	6 +5	9 +5	11 −7	7 +4	13 −8	13 −7

12 −4	12 −3	9 +4	12 −5	6 +8	6 +7	11 −2	4 +9

8 +5	7 +5	11 −4	5 +9	13 −6	12 −5	6 +6	11 −3

12 −7	11 −8	12 −6	13 −9	9 +2	11 −5	12 −9	8 +6

6 +8	8 +3	12 −8	12 −9	5 +9	11 −6

$$\begin{array}{r} 94 \\ -76 \\ \hline \end{array} \qquad \begin{array}{r} 94 \\ -78 \\ \hline \end{array} \qquad \begin{array}{r} 93 \\ -36 \\ \hline \end{array} \qquad \begin{array}{r} 94 \\ -68 \\ \hline \end{array} \qquad \begin{array}{r} 74 \\ -42 \\ \hline \end{array} \qquad \begin{array}{r} 93 \\ -55 \\ \hline \end{array}$$

$$\begin{array}{r} 93 \\ -27 \\ \hline \end{array} \qquad \begin{array}{r} 89 \\ -37 \\ \hline \end{array} \qquad \begin{array}{r} 73 \\ -34 \\ \hline \end{array} \qquad \begin{array}{r} 99 \\ -78 \\ \hline \end{array} \qquad \begin{array}{r} 74 \\ -46 \\ \hline \end{array} \qquad \begin{array}{r} 63 \\ -39 \\ \hline \end{array}$$

$$\begin{array}{r} 62 \\ -24 \\ \hline \end{array} \qquad \begin{array}{r} 83 \\ -26 \\ \hline \end{array} \qquad \begin{array}{r} 54 \\ -38 \\ \hline \end{array} \qquad \begin{array}{r} 99 \\ -67 \\ \hline \end{array} \qquad \begin{array}{r} 64 \\ -38 \\ \hline \end{array} \qquad \begin{array}{r} 54 \\ -36 \\ \hline \end{array}$$

12 things = 1 dozen

6 things = $\frac{1}{2}$ dozen

4	6	4	8	8	6
+9	+8	+9	+5	+6	+6

7	6	9	9	8	8
+5	+7	+5	+4	+6	+5

9	5	4	6	7	9	5	6
+5	+8	+8	+8	+6	+4	+9	+7

5	4	3	4	3	6	3	3
3	2	6	5	4	2	2	4
+5	+8	+4	+5	+6	+6	+8	+5

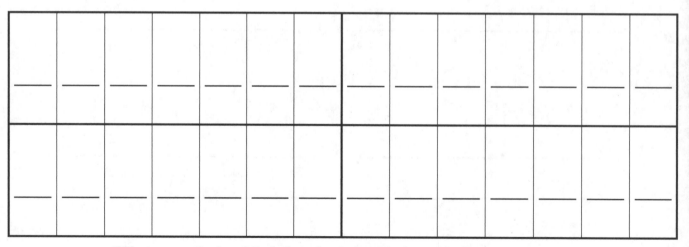

"Whatsoever thy hand findeth to do, do it with thy might." Ecclesiastes 9:10

70

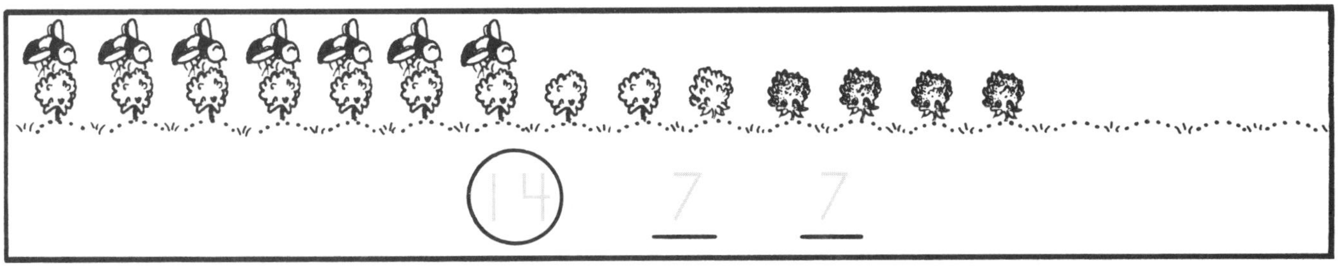

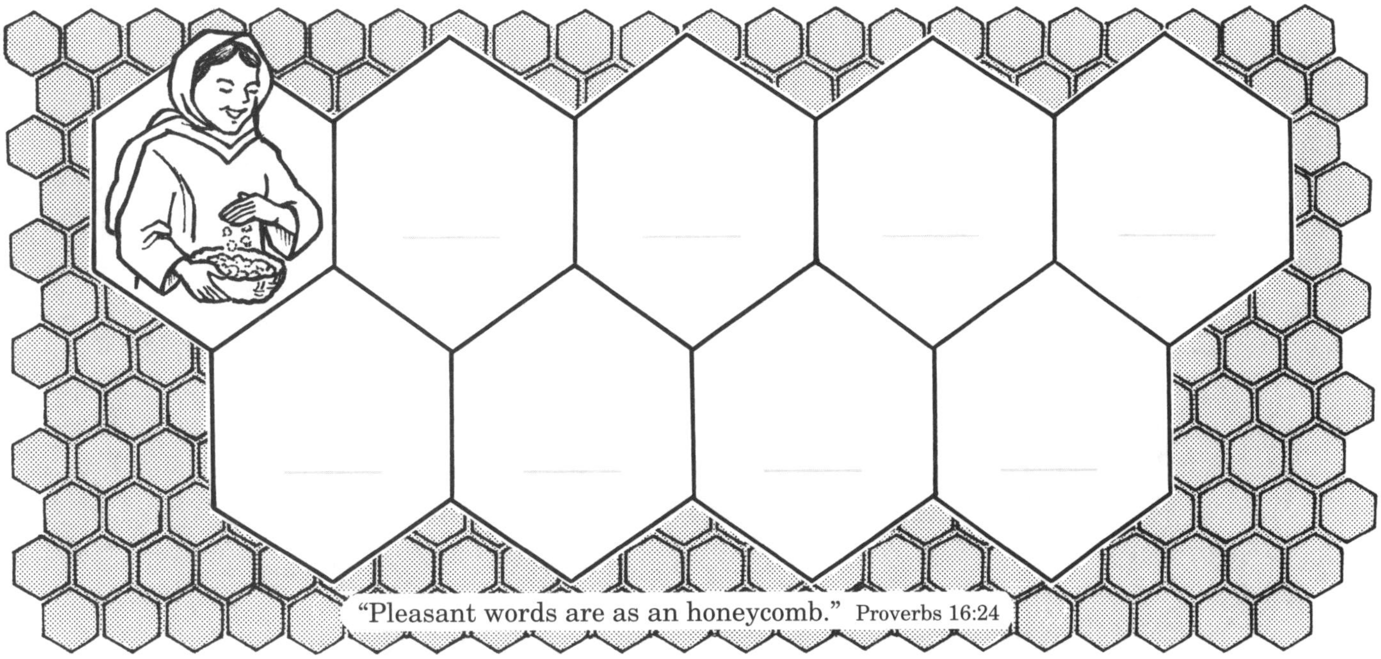

14   7   7

77
14

14   7   14   7
-7 +7 -7 +7

"Pleasant words are as an honeycomb." Proverbs 16:24

71

14	13	13	14	7	14	13	7
-7	-7	-6	-7	+7	-7	-7	+7

7	14	6	7	13	7	14	13
+7	-7	+7	+7	-6	+6	-7	-6

14	13	7	13	7	7	14	6
-7	-6	+7	-7	+6	+7	-7	+7

7	7	14	6	13	14	7	13
+6	+7	-7	+7	-7	-7	+7	-6

14	13	13	14	7	13	14	7
-7	-6	-7	-7	+6	-7	-7	+7

7	6	13	14	7	14
+7	+7	-6	-7	+7	-7

$$\begin{array}{r} 94 \\ -78 \\ \hline \end{array}$$
$$\begin{array}{r} 56 \\ +87 \\ \hline \end{array}$$
$$\begin{array}{r} 84 \\ -66 \\ \hline \end{array}$$
$$\begin{array}{r} 84 \\ -45 \\ \hline \end{array}$$
$$\begin{array}{r} 38 \\ +66 \\ \hline \end{array}$$
$$\begin{array}{r} 64 \\ -29 \\ \hline \end{array}$$

$$\begin{array}{r} 88 \\ +45 \\ \hline \end{array}$$
$$\begin{array}{r} 93 \\ -49 \\ \hline \end{array}$$
$$\begin{array}{r} 46 \\ +77 \\ \hline \end{array}$$
$$\begin{array}{r} 94 \\ -38 \\ \hline \end{array}$$
$$\begin{array}{r} 58 \\ +84 \\ \hline \end{array}$$
$$\begin{array}{r} 93 \\ -54 \\ \hline \end{array}$$

$$\begin{array}{r} 76 \\ +67 \\ \hline \end{array}$$
$$\begin{array}{r} 92 \\ -38 \\ \hline \end{array}$$
$$\begin{array}{r} 94 \\ -48 \\ \hline \end{array}$$
$$\begin{array}{r} 93 \\ -68 \\ \hline \end{array}$$
$$\begin{array}{r} 72 \\ -24 \\ \hline \end{array}$$
$$\begin{array}{r} 78 \\ +65 \\ \hline \end{array}$$

12 things   =   1 dozen

6 things   = $\frac{1}{2}$ dozen

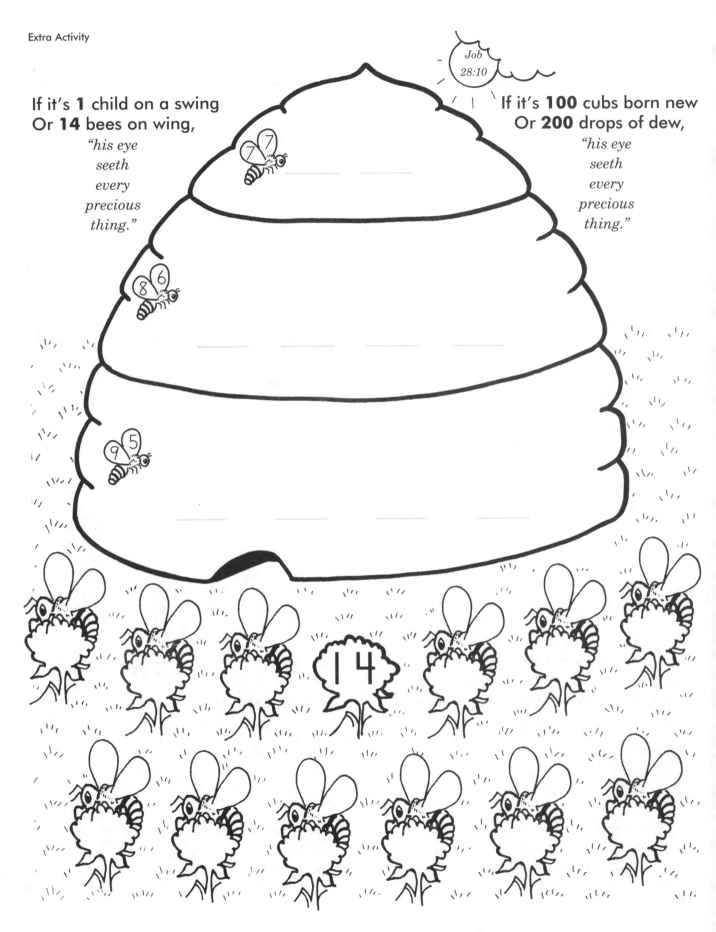

If it's **1** child on a swing
Or **14** bees on wing,

*"his eye
seeth
every
precious
thing."*

Job
28:10

If it's **100** cubs born new
Or **200** drops of dew,

*"his eye
seeth
every
precious
thing."*

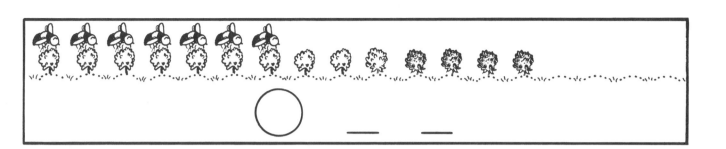

"Pleasant words are as an honeycomb." Proverbs 16:24

144 -73	37 +47	137 -77	148 -74	76 +63	148 -76
37 +67	139 -66	65 +75	149 -74	67 +37	137 -64
139 -79	149 -78	137 -62	149 -75	46 +57	74 +75
138 -65	57 +47	147 -72	70 +70	136 -63	77 +27
149 -77	63 +76	147 -73	135 -75	27 +57	149 -78
		148 -74	138 -63	148 -77	137 -77

Count by

5's

100

14	14	6	14	5	14
-7	-6	+8	-9	+9	-7

14	14	8	7	14	14
-8	-5	+6	+7	-6	-7

6	14	14	8	14	6	14	14
+8	-9	-7	+6	-9	+8	-6	-7

14	7	14	14	9	7	14	14
-9	+7	-7	-6	+5	+7	-5	-8

"Whatsoever thy hand findeth to do, do it with thy might." Ecclesiastes 9:10

78

"Pleasant words are as an honeycomb." Proverbs 16:24

Mother made one dozen buns. The family ate nine of them for dinner. How many buns were left?

At Joy's church there are seven benches on the men's side and 7 benches on the women's side. How many benches is that altogether?

$$
\begin{array}{r} 6 \\ 1 \\ +7 \\ \hline \end{array}
\qquad
\begin{array}{r} 2 \\ 2 \\ +6 \\ \hline \end{array}
\qquad
\begin{array}{r} 3 \\ 6 \\ +4 \\ \hline \end{array}
\qquad
\begin{array}{r} 3 \\ 4 \\ +7 \\ \hline \end{array}
\qquad
\begin{array}{r} 8 \\ 1 \\ +5 \\ \hline \end{array}
\qquad
\begin{array}{r} 5 \\ 2 \\ +7 \\ \hline \end{array}
\qquad
\begin{array}{r} 3 \\ 6 \\ +4 \\ \hline \end{array}
\qquad
\begin{array}{r} 3 \\ 2 \\ +9 \\ \hline \end{array}
$$

$$
\begin{array}{r} 1 \\ 6 \\ +7 \\ \hline \end{array}
\qquad
\begin{array}{r} 7 \\ 2 \\ +2 \\ \hline \end{array}
\qquad
\begin{array}{r} 5 \\ 3 \\ +4 \\ \hline \end{array}
\qquad
\begin{array}{r} 2 \\ 5 \\ +7 \\ \hline \end{array}
\qquad
\begin{array}{r} 4 \\ 3 \\ +7 \\ \hline \end{array}
\qquad
\begin{array}{r} 5 \\ 3 \\ +5 \\ \hline \end{array}
\qquad
\begin{array}{r} 4 \\ 4 \\ +5 \\ \hline \end{array}
\qquad
\begin{array}{r} 7 \\ 0 \\ +7 \\ \hline \end{array}
$$

7 +7	14 −6	14 −8	7 +5	14 −7	4 +9	13 −7	14 −5
13 −9	7 +7	14 −8	6 +8	13 −9	5 +9	8 +6	14 −8
14 −5	13 −7	9 +4	14 −7	5 +7	14 −8	14 −6	6 +8

Count by 5's

100

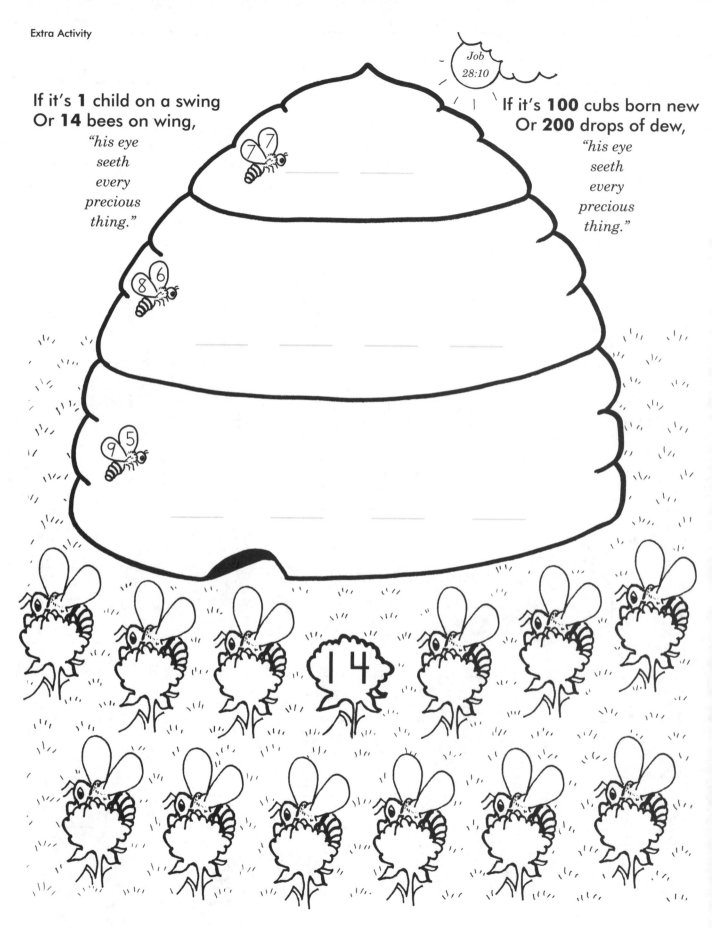

If it's **1** child on a swing
Or **14** bees on wing,

"his eye
seeth
every
precious
thing."

Job 28:10

If it's **100** cubs born new
Or **200** drops of dew,

"his eye
seeth
every
precious
thing."

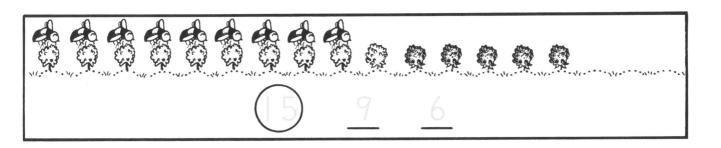

$$15 \quad \underline{} \quad \underline{}$$

$$\begin{array}{cccc} 15 & 15 & 9 & 6 \\ -9 & -6 & +6 & +9 \\ \hline \end{array}$$

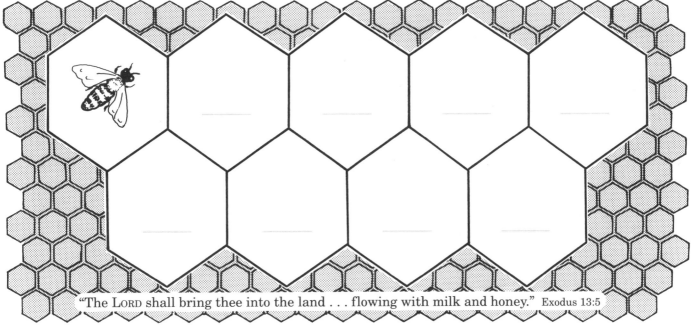

"The LORD shall bring thee into the land . . . flowing with milk and honey." Exodus 13:5

15 −9	15 −6	6 +9	15 −9	15 −6	9 +6

6 +9	15 −6	6 +9	9 +6	15 −6	9 +6	15 −6	15 −9

15 −6	15 −6	9 +6	15 −9	6 +9	6 +9	15 −6	9 +6

6 +9	9 +6	15 −6	9 +6	15 −9	15 −6	6 +9	15 −6

15 −9	15 −6	15 −9	15 −6	9 +6	15 −9	15 −6	9 +6

6 +9	15 −9	9 +6	6 +9	15 −6	9 +6	15 −9	15 −9

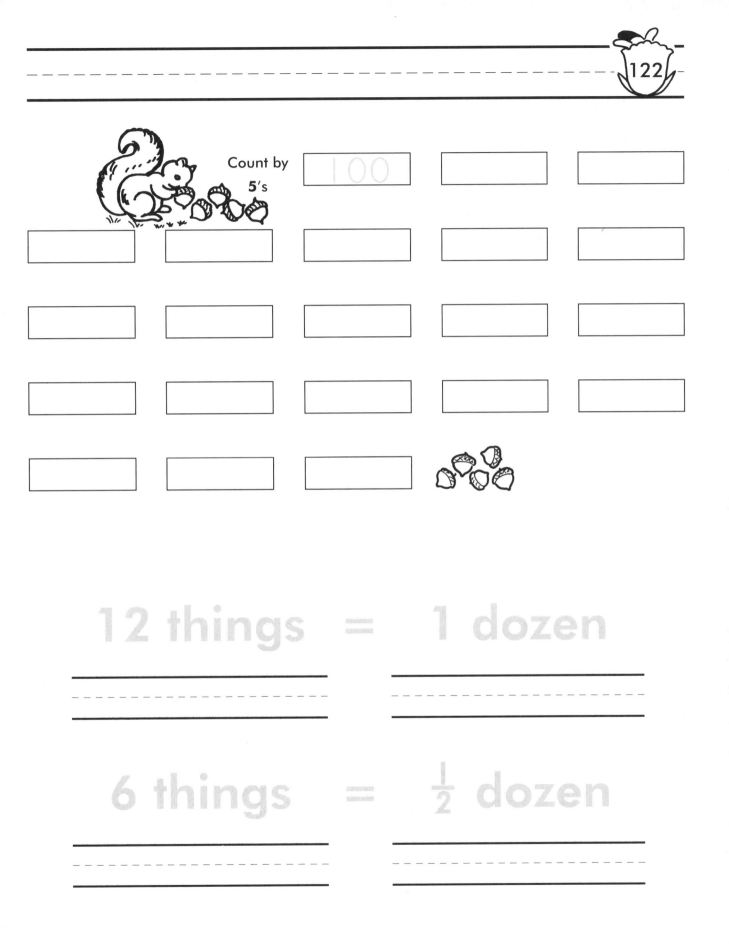

Count by 5's

100

12 things = 1 dozen

6 things = $\frac{1}{2}$ dozen

14	14	14	14	14	14
-5	-7	-9	-8	-6	-9

14	14	14	14	14	14
-5	-8	-9	-5	-8	-9

14	14	14	14	14	14	14	14
-6	-7	-9	-6	-8	-9	-7	-5

4	3	3	2	2	5	4	3
3	4	2	7	6	4	2	5
+7	+5	+8	+5	+6	+4	+6	+6

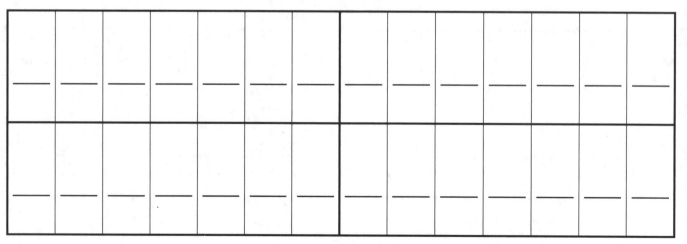

"Whatsoever thy hand findeth to do, do it with thy might." Ecclesiastes 9:10

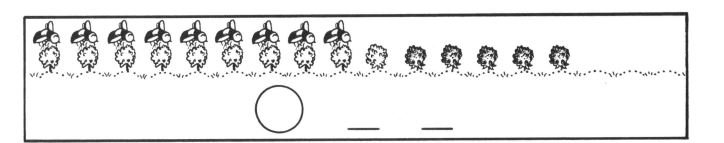

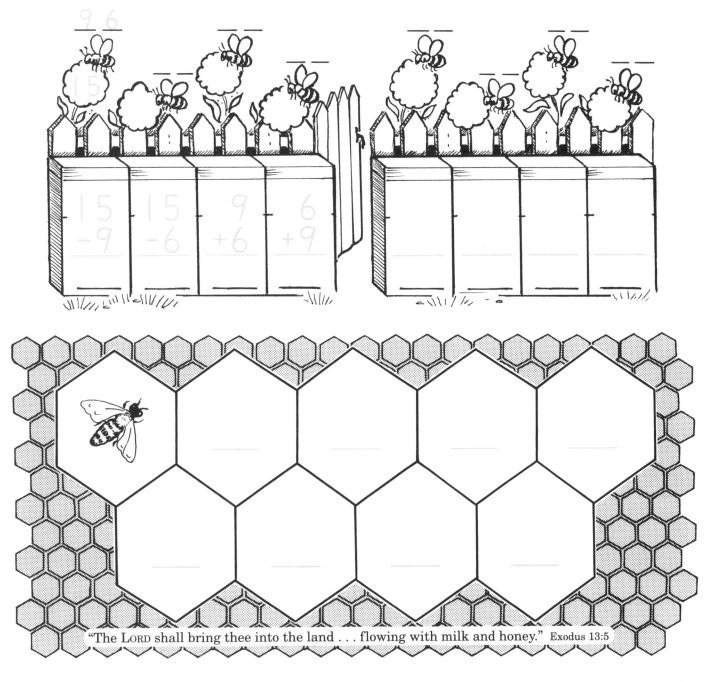

"The LORD shall bring thee into the land . . . flowing with milk and honey." Exodus 13:5

$$\begin{array}{r} 15 \\ -6 \\ \hline \end{array} \quad \begin{array}{r} 15 \\ -9 \\ \hline \end{array} \quad \begin{array}{r} 6 \\ +9 \\ \hline \end{array} \quad \begin{array}{r} 15 \\ -9 \\ \hline \end{array} \quad \begin{array}{r} 15 \\ -6 \\ \hline \end{array} \quad \begin{array}{r} 6 \\ +9 \\ \hline \end{array}$$

$$\begin{array}{r} 9 \\ +6 \\ \hline \end{array} \quad \begin{array}{r} 15 \\ -9 \\ \hline \end{array} \quad \begin{array}{r} 9 \\ +6 \\ \hline \end{array} \quad \begin{array}{r} 6 \\ +9 \\ \hline \end{array} \quad \begin{array}{r} 15 \\ -9 \\ \hline \end{array} \quad \begin{array}{r} 9 \\ +6 \\ \hline \end{array} \quad \begin{array}{r} 15 \\ -9 \\ \hline \end{array} \quad \begin{array}{r} 15 \\ -6 \\ \hline \end{array}$$

$$\begin{array}{r} 15 \\ -9 \\ \hline \end{array} \quad \begin{array}{r} 15 \\ -6 \\ \hline \end{array} \quad \begin{array}{r} 6 \\ +9 \\ \hline \end{array} \quad \begin{array}{r} 15 \\ -9 \\ \hline \end{array} \quad \begin{array}{r} 9 \\ +6 \\ \hline \end{array} \quad \begin{array}{r} 6 \\ +9 \\ \hline \end{array} \quad \begin{array}{r} 15 \\ -6 \\ \hline \end{array} \quad \begin{array}{r} 6 \\ +9 \\ \hline \end{array}$$

$$\begin{array}{r} 9 \\ +6 \\ \hline \end{array} \quad \begin{array}{r} 9 \\ +6 \\ \hline \end{array} \quad \begin{array}{r} 15 \\ -6 \\ \hline \end{array} \quad \begin{array}{r} 9 \\ +6 \\ \hline \end{array} \quad \begin{array}{r} 15 \\ -9 \\ \hline \end{array} \quad \begin{array}{r} 15 \\ -6 \\ \hline \end{array} \quad \begin{array}{r} 9 \\ +6 \\ \hline \end{array} \quad \begin{array}{r} 15 \\ -9 \\ \hline \end{array}$$

$$\begin{array}{r} 15 \\ -9 \\ \hline \end{array} \quad \begin{array}{r} 15 \\ -6 \\ \hline \end{array} \quad \begin{array}{r} 15 \\ -9 \\ \hline \end{array} \quad \begin{array}{r} 15 \\ -6 \\ \hline \end{array} \quad \begin{array}{r} 6 \\ +9 \\ \hline \end{array} \quad \begin{array}{r} 15 \\ -9 \\ \hline \end{array} \quad \begin{array}{r} 15 \\ -6 \\ \hline \end{array} \quad \begin{array}{r} 9 \\ +6 \\ \hline \end{array}$$

$$\begin{array}{r} 9 \\ +6 \\ \hline \end{array} \quad \begin{array}{r} 15 \\ -9 \\ \hline \end{array} \quad \begin{array}{r} 9 \\ +6 \\ \hline \end{array} \quad \begin{array}{r} 6 \\ +9 \\ \hline \end{array} \quad \begin{array}{r} 15 \\ -6 \\ \hline \end{array} \quad \begin{array}{r} 9 \\ +6 \\ \hline \end{array} \quad \begin{array}{r} 15 \\ -9 \\ \hline \end{array} \quad \begin{array}{r} 15 \\ -9 \\ \hline \end{array}$$

$$\begin{array}{r} 259 \\ +383 \\ \hline \end{array}$$
$$\begin{array}{r} 237 \\ +547 \\ \hline \end{array}$$
$$\begin{array}{r} 578 \\ +265 \\ \hline \end{array}$$
$$\begin{array}{r} 445 \\ +489 \\ \hline \end{array}$$
$$\begin{array}{r} 246 \\ +628 \\ \hline \end{array}$$
$$\begin{array}{r} 456 \\ +384 \\ \hline \end{array}$$

$$\begin{array}{r} 437 \\ +267 \\ \hline \end{array}$$
$$\begin{array}{r} 426 \\ +134 \\ \hline \end{array}$$
$$\begin{array}{r} 286 \\ +248 \\ \hline \end{array}$$
$$\begin{array}{r} 307 \\ +397 \\ \hline \end{array}$$
$$\begin{array}{r} 114 \\ +446 \\ \hline \end{array}$$
$$\begin{array}{r} 158 \\ +376 \\ \hline \end{array}$$

$$\begin{array}{r} 583 \\ +257 \\ \hline \end{array}$$
$$\begin{array}{r} 348 \\ +526 \\ \hline \end{array}$$
$$\begin{array}{r} 456 \\ +478 \\ \hline \end{array}$$
$$\begin{array}{r} 489 \\ +354 \\ \hline \end{array}$$
$$\begin{array}{r} 127 \\ +657 \\ \hline \end{array}$$
$$\begin{array}{r} 458 \\ +184 \\ \hline \end{array}$$

Mother made 98 cookies. She gave 65 cookies to a family in need. How many cookies did she have left?

Carl's teacher had one dozen pencils. She gave 8 pencils to the boys and girls. How many pencils did she have left?

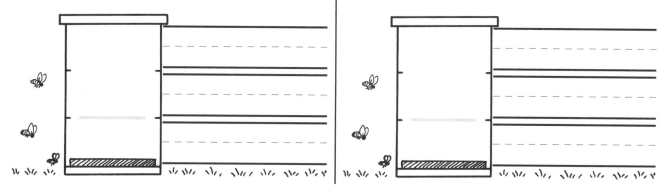

If it's **1** child on a swing
Or **15** bees on wing,

"his eye
seeth
every
precious
thing."

If it's **300** busy ants
Or **400** tiny plants,

"his eye
seeth
every
precious
thing."

Job 28:10

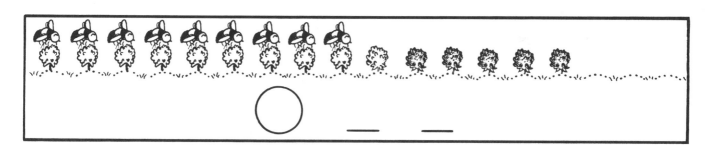

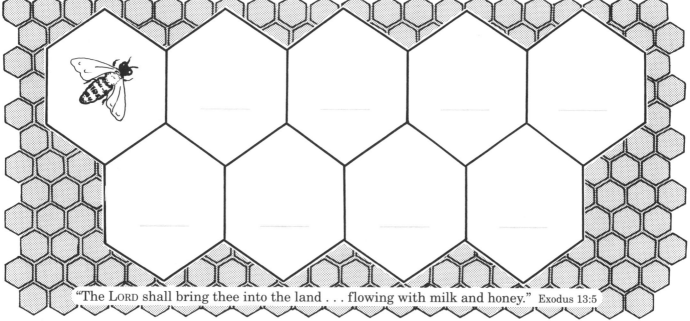

"The LORD shall bring thee into the land . . . flowing with milk and honey." Exodus 13:5

159 −97	158 −63	95 +63	159 −92
66 +29	158 −96	94 +63	159 −64	60 +90	156 −95
83 +67	155 −62	157 −93	158 −67	157 −94	52 +98
159 −98	54 +96	157 −62	95 +62	157 −95	79 +16
155 −93	56 +49	157 −90	60 +98	159 −64	158 −96
86 +64	156 −93	155 −64	156 −92	158 −65	54 +96

$$\begin{array}{r} 9 \\ +6 \\ \hline \end{array} \qquad \begin{array}{r} 14 \\ -7 \\ \hline \end{array} \qquad \begin{array}{r} 15 \\ -9 \\ \hline \end{array} \qquad \begin{array}{r} 6 \\ +9 \\ \hline \end{array} \qquad \begin{array}{r} 14 \\ -8 \\ \hline \end{array} \qquad \begin{array}{r} 6 \\ +8 \\ \hline \end{array} \qquad \begin{array}{r} 13 \\ -7 \\ \hline \end{array} \qquad \begin{array}{r} 14 \\ -6 \\ \hline \end{array}$$

$$\begin{array}{r} 14 \\ -5 \\ \hline \end{array} \qquad \begin{array}{r} 5 \\ +9 \\ \hline \end{array} \qquad \begin{array}{r} 13 \\ -6 \\ \hline \end{array} \qquad \begin{array}{r} 6 \\ +7 \\ \hline \end{array} \qquad \begin{array}{r} 14 \\ -5 \\ \hline \end{array} \qquad \begin{array}{r} 8 \\ +6 \\ \hline \end{array} \qquad \begin{array}{r} 13 \\ -6 \\ \hline \end{array} \qquad \begin{array}{r} 7 \\ +6 \\ \hline \end{array}$$

$$\begin{array}{r} 14 \\ -6 \\ \hline \end{array} \qquad \begin{array}{r} 13 \\ -7 \\ \hline \end{array} \qquad \begin{array}{r} 7 \\ +7 \\ \hline \end{array} \qquad \begin{array}{r} 14 \\ -8 \\ \hline \end{array} \qquad \begin{array}{r} 9 \\ +6 \\ \hline \end{array} \qquad \begin{array}{r} 15 \\ -9 \\ \hline \end{array} \qquad \begin{array}{r} 14 \\ -7 \\ \hline \end{array} \qquad \begin{array}{r} 6 \\ +9 \\ \hline \end{array}$$

15	14	6	15	7	9
-9	-7	+9	-6	+7	+6

9	6	14	7	15	6
+6	+9	-7	+7	-6	+9

15	7	6	7	15	9	14	15
-9	+7	+9	+7	-6	+6	-7	-9

7	15	6	15	7	14	6	9
+7	-9	+9	-6	+7	-7	+9	+6

"Whatsoever thy hand findeth to do, do it with thy might." Ecclesiastes 9:10

"The LORD shall bring thee into the land . . . flowing with milk and honey." Exodus 13:5

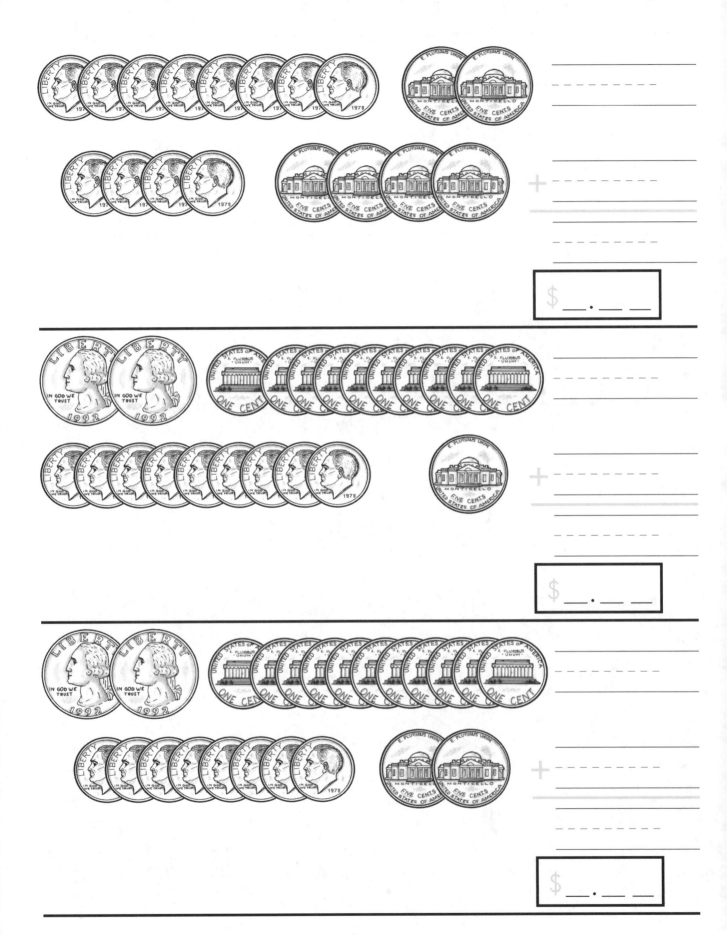

79 +66	85 −76	95 −49	93 −68	62 −54	78 +65
94 −78	56 +87	84 −67	84 −45	38 +66	94 −89
88 +45	74 −67	46 +77	94 −38	58 +84	94 −56

Count by 5's

100		

If it's **1** child on a swing
Or **15** bees on wing,

*"his eye
seeth
every
precious
thing."*

Job 28:10

If it's **300** busy ants
Or **400** tiny plants,

*"his eye
seeth
every
precious
thing."*

"The LORD shall bring thee into the land . . . flowing with milk and honey." Exodus 13:5

$9 + \underline{\quad} = 15$	$15 - \underline{\quad} = 6$	$\underline{\quad} - 6 = 9$
$6 + \underline{\quad} = 15$	$\underline{\quad} + 9 = 15$	$6 + \underline{\quad} = 15$
$15 - \underline{\quad} = 6$	$\underline{\quad} - 9 = 6$	$15 - 9 = \underline{\quad}$
$15 - \underline{\quad} = 9$	$15 - 6 = \underline{\quad}$	$\underline{\quad} - 6 = 9$
$\underline{\quad} + 9 = 15$	$6 + \underline{\quad} = 15$	$6 + \underline{\quad} = 15$
$\underline{\quad} - 9 = 6$	$9 + 6 = \underline{\quad}$	$\underline{\quad} - 9 = 6$

$$\begin{array}{cccccccc} 6 & 7 & 6 & 4 & 8 & 5 & 4 & 1 \\ 3 & 2 & 3 & 5 & 1 & 2 & 2 & 5 \\ +6 & +5 & +4 & +6 & +6 & +6 & +8 & +9 \\ \hline \end{array}$$

$$\begin{array}{cccccccc} 5 & 7 & 2 & 4 & 3 & 3 & 3 & 5 \\ 4 & 2 & 7 & 2 & 3 & 3 & 6 & 1 \\ +6 & +3 & +6 & +8 & +8 & +9 & +3 & +9 \\ \hline \end{array}$$

$$\begin{array}{r} 95 \\ -9 \\ \hline \end{array}$$
$$\begin{array}{r} 94 \\ -8 \\ \hline \end{array}$$
$$\begin{array}{r} 74 \\ -2 \\ \hline \end{array}$$
$$\begin{array}{r} 93 \\ -7 \\ \hline \end{array}$$
$$\begin{array}{r} 94 \\ -7 \\ \hline \end{array}$$
$$\begin{array}{r} 93 \\ -5 \\ \hline \end{array}$$

$$\begin{array}{r} 89 \\ -37 \\ \hline \end{array}$$
$$\begin{array}{r} 94 \\ -88 \\ \hline \end{array}$$
$$\begin{array}{r} 94 \\ -89 \\ \hline \end{array}$$
$$\begin{array}{r} 99 \\ -78 \\ \hline \end{array}$$
$$\begin{array}{r} 74 \\ -48 \\ \hline \end{array}$$
$$\begin{array}{r} 83 \\ -74 \\ \hline \end{array}$$

$$\begin{array}{r} 62 \\ -24 \\ \hline \end{array}$$
$$\begin{array}{r} 55 \\ -39 \\ \hline \end{array}$$
$$\begin{array}{r} 85 \\ -29 \\ \hline \end{array}$$
$$\begin{array}{r} 99 \\ -67 \\ \hline \end{array}$$
$$\begin{array}{r} 64 \\ -38 \\ \hline \end{array}$$
$$\begin{array}{r} 45 \\ -36 \\ \hline \end{array}$$

12 inches = 1 foot

14	15	15	6	14	9
-8	-9	-6	+8	-6	+6

15	9	6	14	15	8
-6	+6	+9	-6	-9	+6

15	6	9	14	6	15	15	14
-9	+9	+6	-6	+8	-6	-9	-8

6	14	8	15	14	9	6	15
+9	-8	+6	-9	-6	+6	+9	-6

"Whatsoever thy hand findeth to do, do it with thy might." Ecclesiastes 9:10

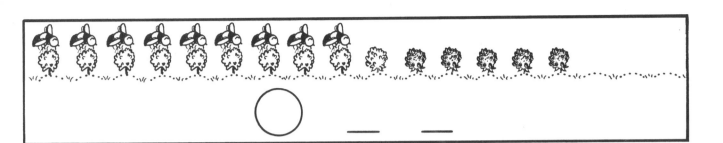

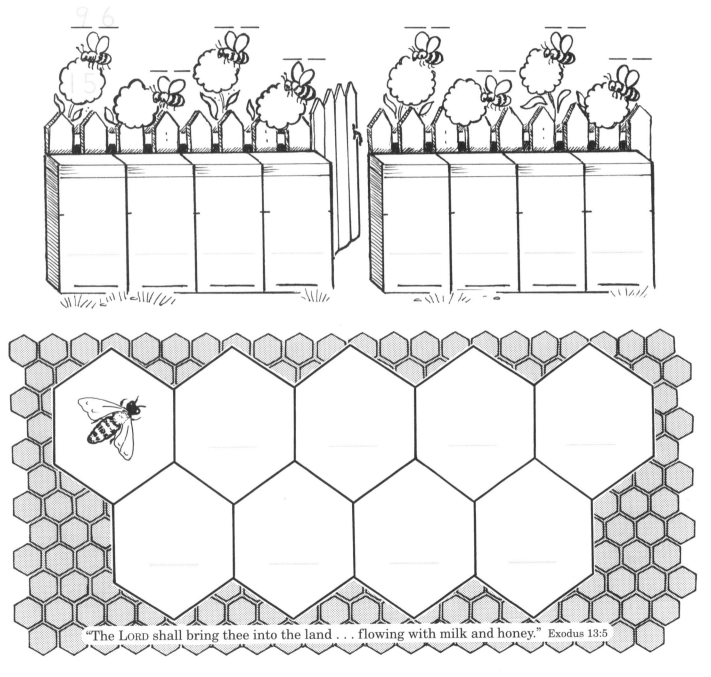

"The LORD shall bring thee into the land . . . flowing with milk and honey." Exodus 13:5

Grandmother gave books to the children. Lee's book has 93 pages. Fay's book has 64 pages. How many pages is that altogether?

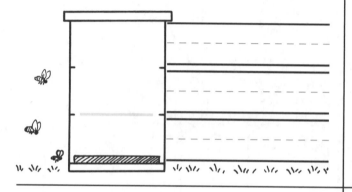

Mother has one dozen oranges in a bag. She gives six of them to Mrs. Gray. How many oranges are in Mother's bag now?

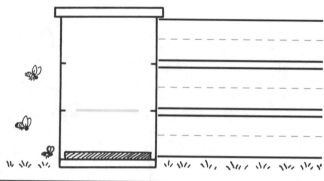

Lois counted fifteen jars on the shelf. Nine jars had beans in them. The rest had peaches. How many jars had peaches?

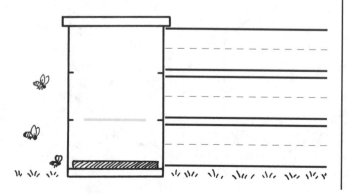

95 ants get into a beehive. 63 ants are coming to the hive. How many ants is that altogether?

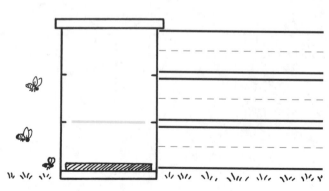

```
  65        94        47        56        94        93
 +78       -78       +96       +78       -55       -36
_____     _____     _____     _____     _____     _____
```

```
  56        65        68        85        69        94
 +99       -56       +76       -76       +55       -29
_____     _____     _____     _____     _____     _____
```

```
  46        84        89        49        75        84
 +97       -65       +56       +86       -36       -27
_____     _____     _____     _____     _____     _____
```

12 inches = 1 foot

If it's **1** child on a swing
Or **15** bees on wing,

"his eye
seeth
every
precious
thing."

Job
28:10

If it's **300** busy ants
Or **400** tiny plants,

"his eye
seeth
every
precious
thing."

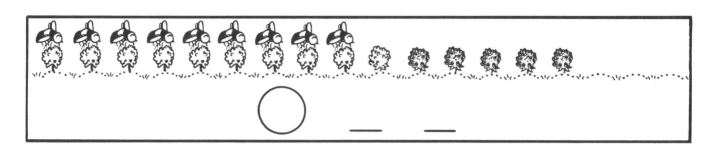

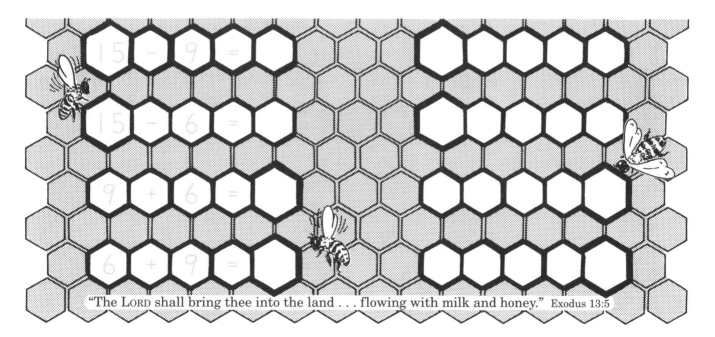

"The LORD shall bring thee into the land . . . flowing with milk and honey." Exodus 13:5

15	15	9	14	15	9
-6	-9	+5	-5	-9	+6

6	14	9	5	15	6	14	15
+9	-9	+6	+9	-9	+9	-9	-6

15	14	6	14	6	9	14	5
-9	-5	+9	-9	+9	+6	-5	+9

9	9	15	9	14	15	6	15
+5	+6	-6	+6	-9	-6	+9	-9

15	14	15	15	9	15	14	5
-6	-9	-6	-9	+5	-6	-9	+9

9	15	9	5	15	6	15	15
+5	-6	+6	+9	-9	+9	-6	-6

56 +99	94 -55	68 +75	85 -76	84 -27	65 +78
56 +78	84 -65	49 +86	94 -78	69 +55	94 -29
75 -36	89 +66	65 -56	47 +96	46 +97	93 -36

12 inches = 1 foot

6	8	9	5	8	6
+9	+5	+6	+9	+6	+9

6	7	6	5	4	6
+7	+7	+9	+9	+9	+7

8	5	9	9	6	6	7	9
+6	+8	+6	+5	+8	+9	+6	+6

6	3	4	3	2	4	2	5
2	6	4	4	5	2	4	3
+5	+5	+5	+6	+7	+9	+8	+5

"Whatsoever thy hand findeth to do, do it with thy might." Ecclesiastes 9:10

○   __ __

9 6
15

15 − 9 =
15 − 6 =
9 + 6 =
6 + 9 =

"The LORD shall bring thee into the land . . . flowing with milk and honey."   Exodus 13:5

15 −9	12 −4	6 +9	14 −5	12 −6	7 +7

6 +8	14 −9	6 +6	9 +6	13 −5	5 +7	13 −8	13 −7

13 −6	13 −9	6 +7	14 −7	9 +5	5 +8	12 −8	6 +9

9 +6	3 +9	13 −4	5 +9	14 −7	15 −6	4 +8	12 −5

12 −7	15 −6	14 −8	12 −4	4 +9	15 −9	12 −3	5 +9

8 +6	12 −9	7 +6	8 +5	14 −6	6 +7	12 −9	14 −9

```
  15      63      22      62      36      47
  23      34      37      23      22      41
 +94     +42     +85     +54     +55     +45
_____  _____  _____  _____  _____  _____


  66      54      33      44      23      55
  23      32      44      22      66      33
 +46     +63     +57     +53     +44     +46
_____  _____  _____  _____  _____  _____
```

3 feet   =   1 yard

If it's **1** child on a swing
Or **15** bees on wing,

*"his eye
seeth
every
precious
thing."*

*Job
28:10*

If it's **300** busy ants
Or **400** tiny plants,

*"his eye
seeth
every
precious
thing."*

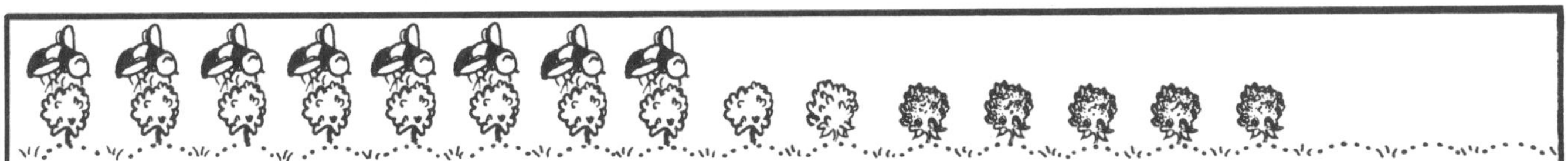

15   8   7

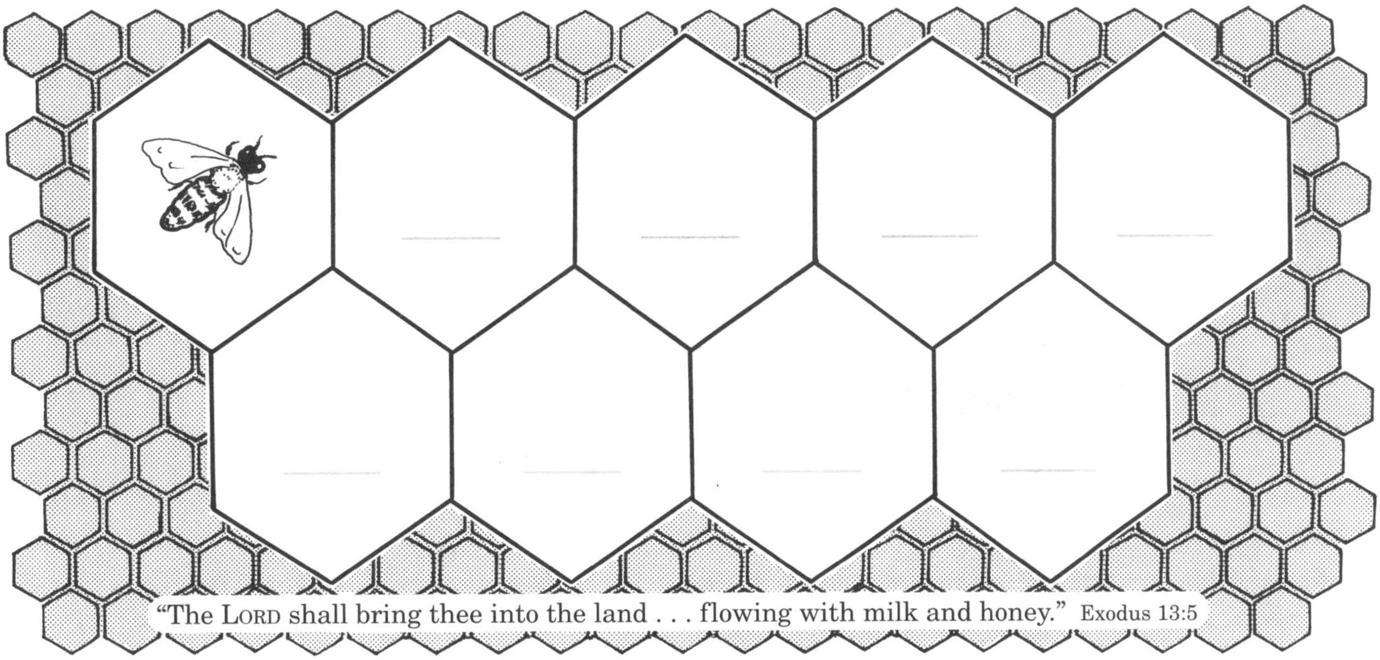

8 7

15

$$\begin{array}{r}15\\-8\\\hline\end{array}$$ $$\begin{array}{r}15\\-7\\\hline\end{array}$$ $$\begin{array}{r}8\\+7\\\hline\end{array}$$ $$\begin{array}{r}7\\+8\\\hline\end{array}$$

"The LORD shall bring thee into the land . . . flowing with milk and honey." Exodus 13:5

$$\begin{array}{r} 15 \\ -8 \\ \hline \end{array} \quad \begin{array}{r} 15 \\ -7 \\ \hline \end{array} \quad \begin{array}{r} 7 \\ +8 \\ \hline \end{array} \quad \begin{array}{r} 15 \\ -8 \\ \hline \end{array} \quad \begin{array}{r} 15 \\ -7 \\ \hline \end{array} \quad \begin{array}{r} 8 \\ +7 \\ \hline \end{array}$$

$$\begin{array}{r} 7 \\ +8 \\ \hline \end{array} \quad \begin{array}{r} 15 \\ -8 \\ \hline \end{array} \quad \begin{array}{r} 8 \\ +7 \\ \hline \end{array} \quad \begin{array}{r} 7 \\ +8 \\ \hline \end{array} \quad \begin{array}{r} 15 \\ -7 \\ \hline \end{array} \quad \begin{array}{r} 7 \\ +8 \\ \hline \end{array} \quad \begin{array}{r} 15 \\ -8 \\ \hline \end{array} \quad \begin{array}{r} 15 \\ -8 \\ \hline \end{array}$$

$$\begin{array}{r} 15 \\ -7 \\ \hline \end{array} \quad \begin{array}{r} 15 \\ -7 \\ \hline \end{array} \quad \begin{array}{r} 7 \\ +8 \\ \hline \end{array} \quad \begin{array}{r} 15 \\ -8 \\ \hline \end{array} \quad \begin{array}{r} 8 \\ +7 \\ \hline \end{array} \quad \begin{array}{r} 7 \\ +8 \\ \hline \end{array} \quad \begin{array}{r} 15 \\ -7 \\ \hline \end{array} \quad \begin{array}{r} 7 \\ +8 \\ \hline \end{array}$$

$$\begin{array}{r} 8 \\ +7 \\ \hline \end{array} \quad \begin{array}{r} 7 \\ +8 \\ \hline \end{array} \quad \begin{array}{r} 15 \\ -8 \\ \hline \end{array} \quad \begin{array}{r} 7 \\ +8 \\ \hline \end{array} \quad \begin{array}{r} 15 \\ -8 \\ \hline \end{array} \quad \begin{array}{r} 15 \\ -8 \\ \hline \end{array} \quad \begin{array}{r} 8 \\ +7 \\ \hline \end{array} \quad \begin{array}{r} 15 \\ -7 \\ \hline \end{array}$$

$$\begin{array}{r} 15 \\ -8 \\ \hline \end{array} \quad \begin{array}{r} 15 \\ -7 \\ \hline \end{array} \quad \begin{array}{r} 15 \\ -8 \\ \hline \end{array} \quad \begin{array}{r} 15 \\ -7 \\ \hline \end{array} \quad \begin{array}{r} 8 \\ +7 \\ \hline \end{array} \quad \begin{array}{r} 15 \\ -8 \\ \hline \end{array} \quad \begin{array}{r} 15 \\ -7 \\ \hline \end{array} \quad \begin{array}{r} 15 \\ -8 \\ \hline \end{array}$$

$$\begin{array}{r} 15 \\ -8 \\ \hline \end{array} \quad \begin{array}{r} 15 \\ -7 \\ \hline \end{array} \quad \begin{array}{r} 8 \\ +7 \\ \hline \end{array} \quad \begin{array}{r} 7 \\ +8 \\ \hline \end{array} \quad \begin{array}{r} 15 \\ -7 \\ \hline \end{array} \quad \begin{array}{r} 7 \\ +8 \\ \hline \end{array} \quad \begin{array}{r} 15 \\ -7 \\ \hline \end{array} \quad \begin{array}{r} 15 \\ -8 \\ \hline \end{array}$$

$$\begin{array}{r} 95 \\ -79 \\ \hline \end{array} \qquad \begin{array}{r} 99 \\ -69 \\ \hline \end{array} \qquad \begin{array}{r} 83 \\ -44 \\ \hline \end{array} \qquad \begin{array}{r} 99 \\ -35 \\ \hline \end{array} \qquad \begin{array}{r} 83 \\ -37 \\ \hline \end{array} \qquad \begin{array}{r} 95 \\ -66 \\ \hline \end{array}$$

$$\begin{array}{r} 94 \\ -27 \\ \hline \end{array} \qquad \begin{array}{r} 73 \\ -48 \\ \hline \end{array} \qquad \begin{array}{r} 99 \\ -56 \\ \hline \end{array} \qquad \begin{array}{r} 83 \\ -16 \\ \hline \end{array} \qquad \begin{array}{r} 64 \\ -39 \\ \hline \end{array} \qquad \begin{array}{r} 78 \\ -35 \\ \hline \end{array}$$

$$\begin{array}{r} 84 \\ -55 \\ \hline \end{array} \qquad \begin{array}{r} 95 \\ -49 \\ \hline \end{array} \qquad \begin{array}{r} 88 \\ -24 \\ \hline \end{array} \qquad \begin{array}{r} 95 \\ -56 \\ \hline \end{array} \qquad \begin{array}{r} 87 \\ -57 \\ \hline \end{array} \qquad \begin{array}{r} 84 \\ -68 \\ \hline \end{array}$$

3 feet   =   1 yard

15	14	14	14	15	14
-9	-7	-6	-9	-6	-5

15	14	14	14	14	14
-6	-8	-7	-5	-6	-9

15	14	15	14	14	14	14	15
-9	-5	-9	-7	-6	-9	-5	-6

15	14	14	14	15	14	15	15
-6	-8	-9	-6	-6	-7	-9	-6

"Whatsoever thy hand findeth to do, do it with thy might." Ecclesiastes 9:10

$\bigcirc$ ___   ___

$$
\begin{array}{cccc}
15 & 15 & 8 & 7 \\
-8 & -7 & +7 & +8 \\
\hline
\end{array}
$$

"The LORD shall bring thee into the land . . . flowing with milk and honey." Exodus 13:5

| | 15
−7 | 15
−8 | 8
+7 | 15
−8 | 15
−7 | 15
−7 |

| 15
−7 | 15
−8 | 8
+7 | 7
+8 | 15
−8 | 7
+8 | 15
−8 | 15
−7 |

| 15
−8 | 15
−7 | 8
+7 | 15
−7 | 7
+8 | 7
+8 | 15
−7 | 8
+7 |

| 7
+8 | 8
+7 | 15
−8 | 8
+7 | 15
−7 | 15
−8 | 7
+8 | 15
−8 |

| 15
−7 | 15
−8 | 15
−7 | 15
−8 | 7
+8 | 15
−7 | 15
−8 | 8
+7 |

| 7
+8 | 15
−8 | 7
+8 | 8
+7 | 15
−8 | 8
+7 | 15
−8 | 15
−7 |

579	337	266	436	355	387
+366	+367	+529	+358	+449	+366

485	576	349	257	179	118
+269	+369	+355	+497	+766	+586

268	266	525	359	454	126
+436	+679	+269	+436	+299	+678

3 feet   =   1 yard

Job 28:10

If it's **1** child on a swing
Or **15** bees on wing,
*"his eye
seeth
every
precious
thing."*

If it's **300** busy ants
Or **400** tiny plants,
*"his eye
seeth
every
precious
thing."*

8 7

9 6

15

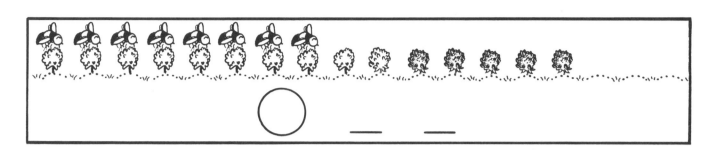

$\bigcirc$ ___   ___

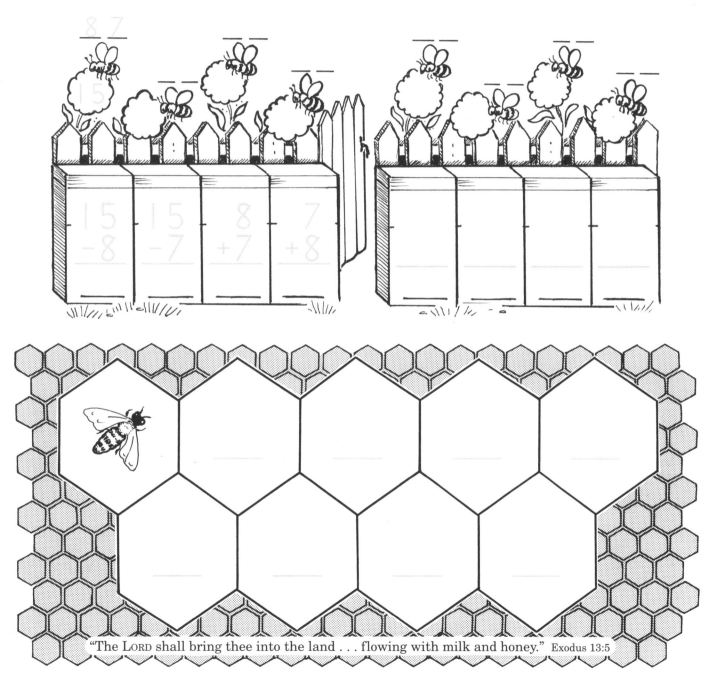

8 7

15

| 15 | 15 | 8 | 7 |
| −8 | −7 | +7 | +8 |

"The LORD shall bring thee into the land . . . flowing with milk and honey." Exodus 13:5

159 −87	158 −73	85 +73	159 −82

78 +37	158 −86	74 +83	159 −74	80 +70	156 −85

68 +87	155 −72	157 −83	158 −77	157 −84	77 +48

159 −88	74 +76	157 −72	85 +72	157 −85	67 +48

155 −73	68 +67	157 −80	70 +88	159 −74	158 −86

68 +57	156 −83	155 −74	156 −82	158 −75	77 +78

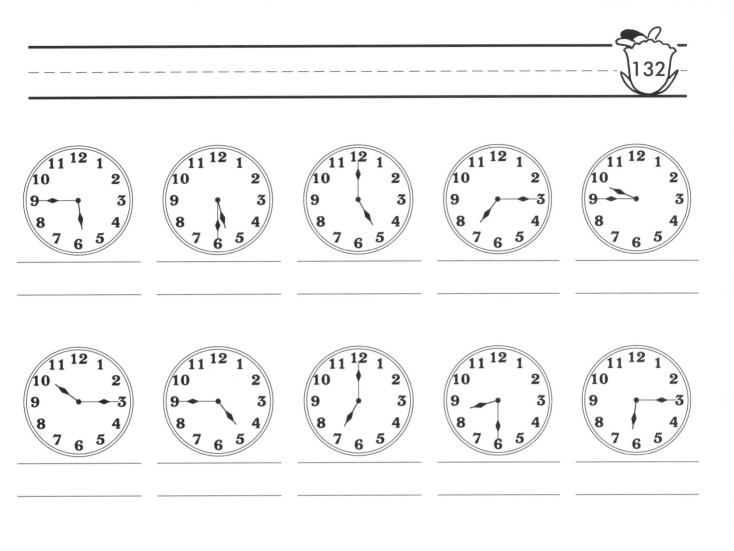

12 inches = 1 foot

3 feet = 1 yard

8	15	15	9	15	15
+7	-8	-9	+6	-6	-7

7	6	15	8	15	15
+8	+9	-6	+7	-7	-9

15	9	15	15	7	15	15	8
-8	+6	-7	-6	+8	-9	-8	+7

8	15	15	15	8	15	9	7
+7	-8	-9	-7	+7	-6	+6	+8

"Whatsoever thy hand findeth to do, do it with thy might." Ecclesiastes 9:10

126

"The LORD shall bring thee into the land . . . flowing with milk and honey." Exodus 13:5

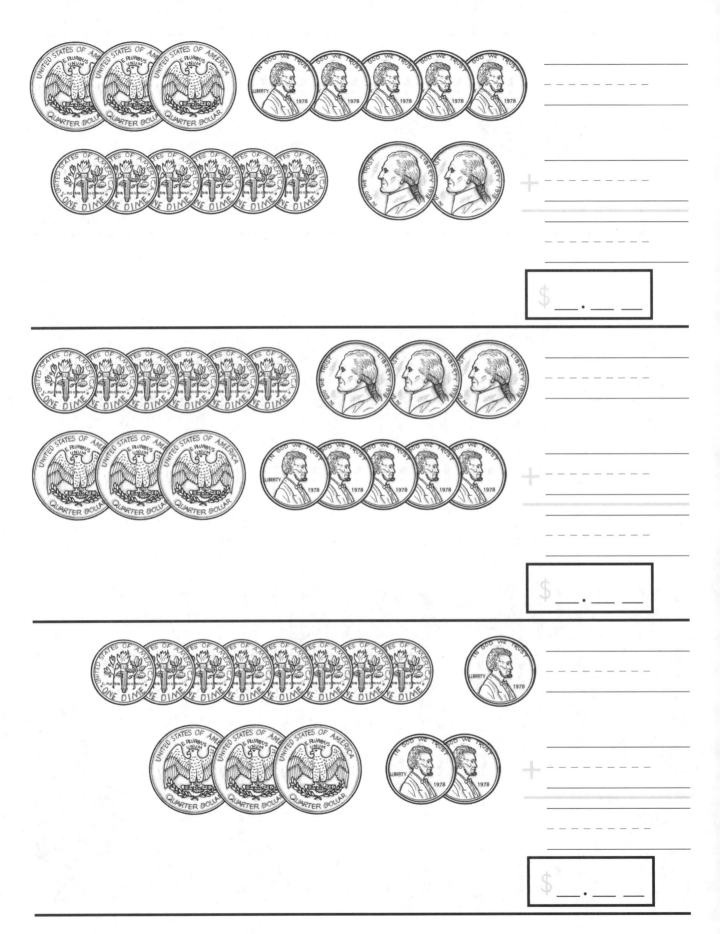

$$\begin{array}{r} 78 \\ +67 \\ \hline \end{array}$$ $$\begin{array}{r} 77 \\ +76 \\ \hline \end{array}$$ $$\begin{array}{r} 95 \\ -59 \\ \hline \end{array}$$ $$\begin{array}{r} 95 \\ -68 \\ \hline \end{array}$$ $$\begin{array}{r} 77 \\ +68 \\ \hline \end{array}$$ $$\begin{array}{r} 95 \\ -37 \\ \hline \end{array}$$

$$\begin{array}{r} 95 \\ -68 \\ \hline \end{array}$$ $$\begin{array}{r} 47 \\ +98 \\ \hline \end{array}$$ $$\begin{array}{r} 95 \\ -57 \\ \hline \end{array}$$ $$\begin{array}{r} 84 \\ -57 \\ \hline \end{array}$$ $$\begin{array}{r} 66 \\ +79 \\ \hline \end{array}$$ $$\begin{array}{r} 85 \\ -47 \\ \hline \end{array}$$

$$\begin{array}{r} 85 \\ -58 \\ \hline \end{array}$$ $$\begin{array}{r} 74 \\ -38 \\ \hline \end{array}$$ $$\begin{array}{r} 85 \\ +68 \\ \hline \end{array}$$ $$\begin{array}{r} 67 \\ +78 \\ \hline \end{array}$$ $$\begin{array}{r} 85 \\ -27 \\ \hline \end{array}$$ $$\begin{array}{r} 86 \\ +59 \\ \hline \end{array}$$

12 inches = 1 foot

3 feet = 1 yard

If it's **1** child on a swing
Or **15** bees on wing,
"his eye seeth every precious thing."

If it's **300** busy ants
Or **400** tiny plants,
"his eye seeth every precious thing."

Job 28:10

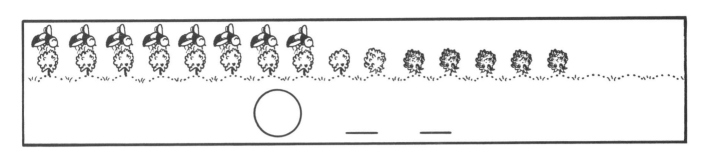

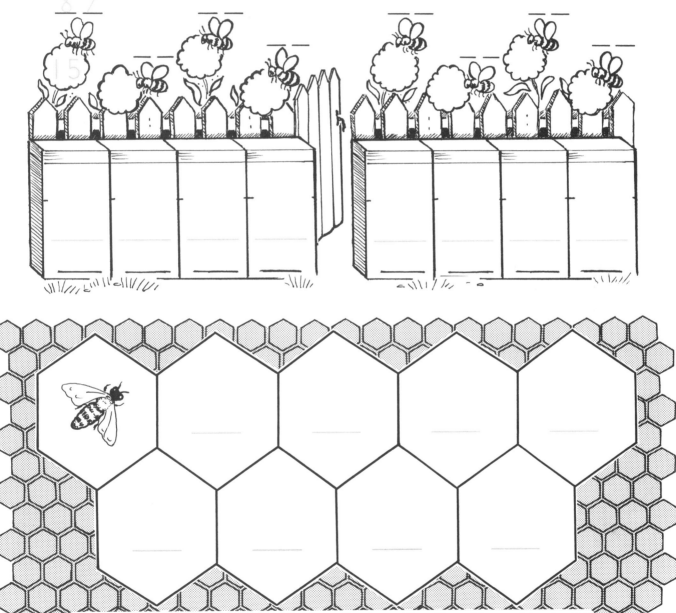

"The Lord shall bring thee into the land . . . flowing with milk and honey." Exodus 13:5

8 + 7 = ___	15 - ___ = 8	8 + 7 = ___
15 - 7 = ___	15 - 8 = ___	15 - 7 = ___
15 - ___ = 7	7 + 8 = ___	___ - 8 = 7
___ + 8 = 15	8 + ___ = 15	7 + 8 = ___
15 - ___ = 7	___ + 7 = 15	8 + ___ = 15
___ + 8 = 15	15 - ___ = 8	___ - 7 = 8

$$\begin{array}{cccccccc} 4 & 7 & 4 & 2 & 3 & 7 & 2 & 7 \\ 4 & 2 & 3 & 6 & 5 & 2 & 6 & 0 \\ +7 & +5 & +8 & +7 & +7 & +4 & +4 & +8 \\ \hline \end{array}$$

$$\begin{array}{cccccccc} 5 & 3 & 6 & 6 & 3 & 5 & 1 & 3 \\ 4 & 4 & 2 & 1 & 3 & 3 & 6 & 5 \\ +5 & +8 & +7 & +8 & +7 & +7 & +8 & +4 \\ \hline \end{array}$$

8 +7	15 −8	15 −9	6 +9	14 −8	7 +8	14 −5	14 −6

15 −8	5 +8	15 −7	8 +7	15 −8	6 +7	7 +8	15 −7

15 −7	15 −6	8 +7	13 −7	7 +8	15 −9	14 −7	6 +9

12 inches = 1 foot

_____

3 feet = 1 yard

_____

15	14	8	7	15	14
-8	-8	+6	+8	-7	-6

8	6	14	14	15	7
+7	+8	-8	-6	-8	+8

15	8	15	14	8	8	14	15
-7	+7	-7	-6	+7	+6	-8	-8

7	14	7	15	15	14	6	8
+8	-6	+8	-8	-7	-8	+8	+7

"Whatsoever thy hand findeth to do, do it with thy might." Ecclesiastes 9:10

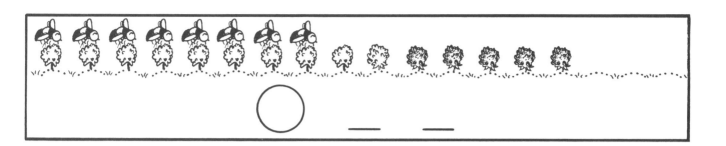

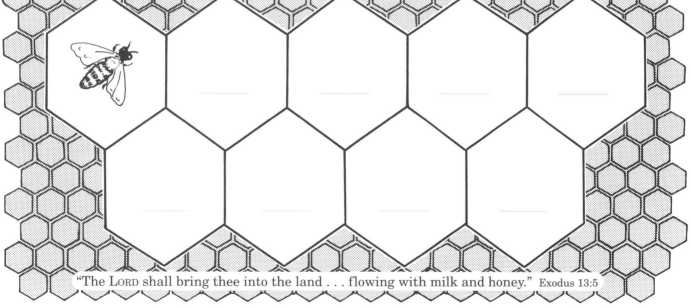

"The LORD shall bring thee into the land . . . flowing with milk and honey." Exodus 13:5

God sent a wind. It did what we could not do. It blew down 7 trees in the woods. It blew down 8 trees in the fields. How many trees was that?

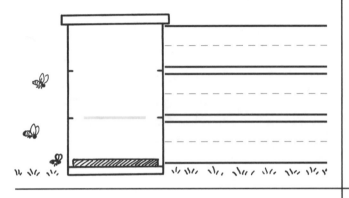

Fifteen kites sail up into the sky. Then 7 kites drop down to the ground. How many kites are left in the sky?

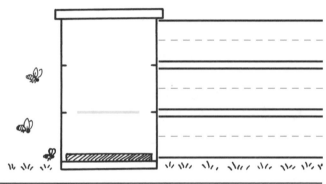

Fred's pet duck has one dozen eggs in her nest. 7 eggs hatch. How many eggs do not hatch?

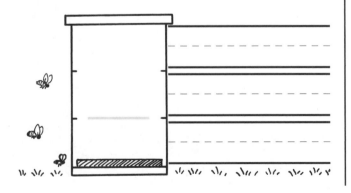

Father pays 38¢ for a pencil and 57¢ for a pen. How many cents does Father pay for both things?

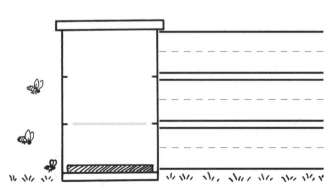

65 − 8	58 + 7	85 − 7	64 − 5	35 − 9	64 − 7
88 +47	95 −48	56 +79	67 +68	73 −66	47 +88
65 −58	64 −38	95 −36	95 −17	26 +39	95 −38

If it's **1** child on a swing
Or **15** bees on wing,

*"his eye
seeth
every
precious
thing."*

If it's **300** busy ants
Or **400** tiny plants,

*"his eye
seeth
every
precious
thing."*

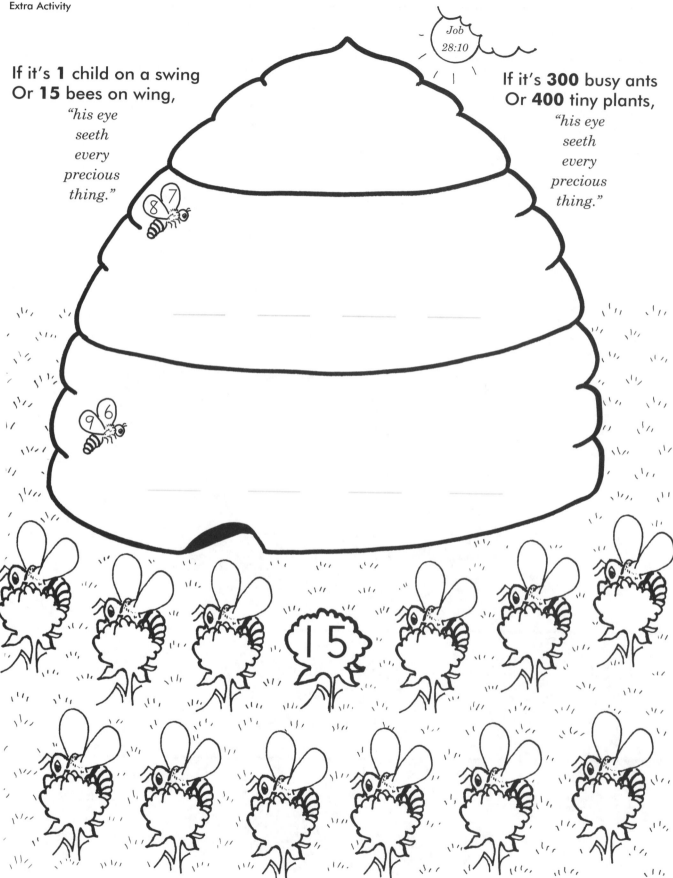

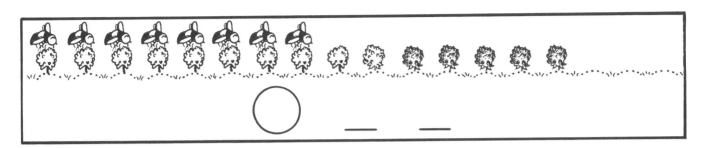

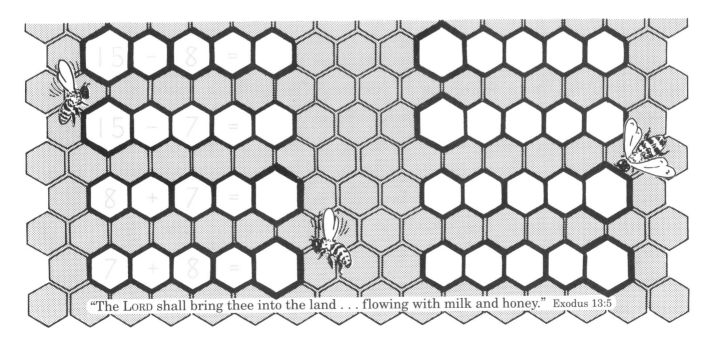

"The Lord shall bring thee into the land . . . flowing with milk and honey." Exodus 13:5

	15 −8	14 −6	7 +8	15 −8	15 −7	8 +7
7 +8	14 −8	6 +8	7 +8	15 −7	8 +6	14 −8	15 −8
14 −8	15 −7	7 +8	14 −6	6 +8	7 +8	14 −6	6 +8
8 +6	7 +8	15 −8	8 +6	15 −7	15 −8	8 +7	14 −8
14 −8	15 −7	15 −8	14 −6	8 +7	15 −8	15 −7	15 −8
15 −8	15 −7	8 +6	7 +8	15 −7	6 +8	14 −6	14 −8

45	78	85	65	35	24
− 8	+ 7	− 6	− 7	− 9	− 7

78	55	56	57	74	57
+47	−47	+89	+68	−56	+88

65	64	95	95	46	85
−38	−38	−37	−16	+39	−78

Speed Drill

8 +7	5 +9	6 +7	9 +6	8 +5	6 +8

9 +4	7 +8	8 +6	7 +7	8 +7	9 +5

6 +7	8 +7	9 +5	5 +8	9 +6	7 +6	6 +8	6 +9

4 2 +9	4 4 +5	3 4 +7	2 5 +8	5 3 +6	3 2 +9	2 6 +7	3 1 +9

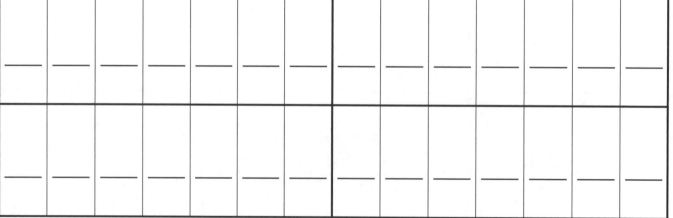

"Whatsoever thy hand findeth to do, do it with thy might." Ecclesiastes 9:10

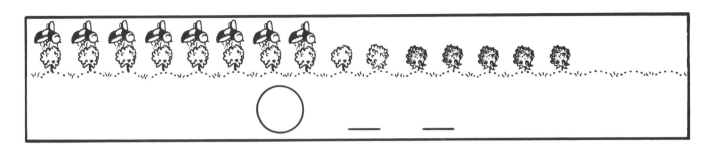

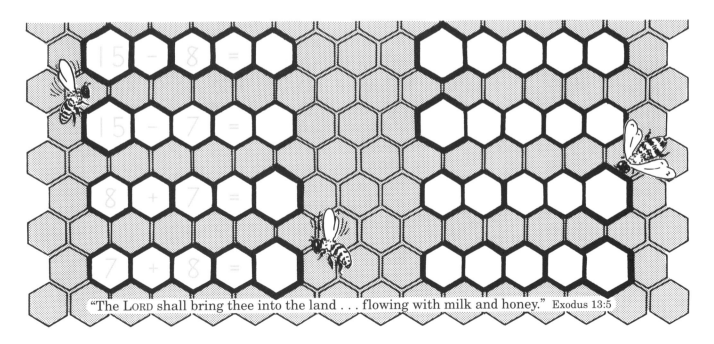

"The LORD shall bring thee into the land . . . flowing with milk and honey." Exodus 13:5

15 −7	15 −8	7 +6	15 −8	15 −7	15 −9

14 −8	15 −8	8 +7	5 +8	15 −8	7 +8	14 −7	15 −7

15 −8	13 −4	5 +7	15 −6	6 +7	4 +8	15 −6	6 +8

5 +9	9 +4	15 −8	5 +8	14 −5	13 −6	8 +5	15 −8

14 −6	14 −9	13 −5	15 −8	6 +9	15 −7	13 −8	7 +7

9 +5	13 −7	7 +8	9 +6	15 −8	8 +7	15 −9	15 −7

Mother made one dozen pies. She took 8 pies to an all-day church meeting. How many pies did she have left?

Lois makes 18 cookies to look like rabbits. Fay makes 27 cookies to look like ducks. How many cookies do both girls make?

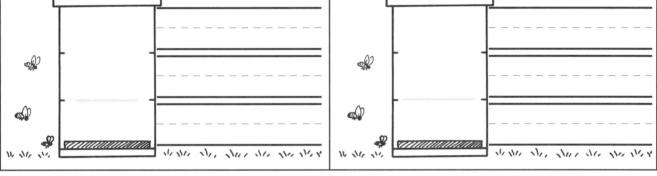

145

If it's **1** child on a swing
Or **15** bees on wing,

*"his eye
seeth
every
precious
thing."*

*Job
28:10*

If it's **300** busy ants
Or **400** tiny plants,

*"his eye
seeth
every
precious
thing."*